BEARDS DON'T GROW IN HEAVEN

UNVEILING TOMORROW'S GENIUS

Oche Itodo

A catalogue for this book is available at the National Library of Nigeria.

E-mail: oche@ocheitodo.com
Website: www.ocheitodo.com

ISBN: 978-978-993-659-5

Cover design/Layout by:
jamesbrown.19.sa@gmail.com
Tel: 08119719710

Published under the imprint of
The African Culture Club Writers
Woji Portharcourt Nigeria.
+2348064300836
africancultureclubwriters@gmail.com

CONTENTS

DEDICATION
Preface
Foreword

01 The Butterfly Generation

02 Looking Beyond Religion's Iron Curtain

03 The Almajiri-Trapped Behind Religion's Iron Curtain

04 The Butchers of the World-Education

05 Erasing the Gender Dichotomy

06 The Right to Play

07 Little Drowning Voices in a World that won't Stop Impaling Gay People

08 Artificial Intelligence, Transhumanism and Children

09 The Environmental Conundrum

10 Crime, Children, and the Death Penalty

11 The Future of Africa and its Children in the World

Epilogue
Afterword
Acknowledgements
Bibliography

Light in darkness
Darkness in light
Fury of humans

Through threads woven
Through hearts entwined
Seeing but groping
On the way we found

Truth in lies
Lies in truth
Joy of living
Happiness untold

Liberty and bondage bound
From the mesh we choose
Freedom untold awaits

On the other side
'Tis light that wins.

- Oche Itodo

DEDICATION

———

To Abdulkadir, the young Almajiri boy who gave me hope, and a different perspective on vulnerability and poverty in my time of distress. I hope he fulfils his promise.

PREFACE

If you wonder, like I do, why we confront the same problem with the same level of thinking that created them, you have just picked up the right book. Growing up as children, most of us had a pinch of fear instilled by nature to keep us safe, but I quickly learned that the fear in our eyes is always a veil that stands between us and our destinations.

This veil blocks the tunnel that leads to our ultimate desired goals in life. The fear comes not from what may lie behind the veil itself but from a glowing ignorance of what awaits us behind it. But like many men and women who have conquered one fear or another and have moved on towards the actualization of their goals happily, what lies behind this veil almost always serves to make us better humans. And painlessly so!

Children are the foundation of tomorrow. They possess potentials within them as an acorn holds within its unbroken shell, a giant oak tree. We can speculate all we want, but we would never know how tall the oak tree will be if we do not release it into the soil and tend carefully to it, ensuring that it receives adequate nutrients, water, and sunlight. The veil of fear tortures us and prevents us from providing these necessary resources to children, which serves to promote the full expression of their potentials.

Yet, to have a progressive world which we seem to be working so hard at delivering to these young ones, we must cast this veil of fear aside and begin to act before we lose the window of opportunity to build the world that visionaries from the past have envisioned.

Moved by my personal experiences and belief in childhood's sanctity and the hope that children represent, I chose to write this book slowly over six years. This seems like a long time, and I indeed should have completed it earlier and released it to the world were it not for the many interruptive journeys that my studies across different continents subjected me to. I still think that it was a blessing in disguise because I have been able to interact with children from different origins in the world-in rural villages and cosmopolitan cities from whom I learned a lot of the lessons and aspirations I share in this book. Some of them have voiced their hopes for the future to me expressly in words, while many others have made their point in the way they choose to live at the dawn of their lives.

I am not a child psychologist, but I believe that my experiences and passion for an avant-garde and resilient generation of children lends credence to my voice on the issues discussed in this book. I have been interested in advocating for human rights, which morphed from my interest in child rights more than a decade ago along with my dear friend Felix Ubani. I have also been a contributor to global development in the little ways that my current expertise as an epidemiologist and international health expert permits. My experiences as a child growing up even in the midst of the deprivation of resources, but blessed with the richness of African culture are some of the cardinal points that moved me to write this book which I hope from the depths of my heart that you will enjoy.

Oche Itodo, March 2021

FOREWORD

"No man who is unwilling to persevere to the end in the nurture and education of children should bring children into this world." **The above instance makes a defined rule by the ancient and renowned early Greek philosopher, Plato.**

When I was commissioned to write this introduction, it felt uneasy and tremendous in a sense, I feel grateful and opportune to be amongst the very few who had access or came in contact with the early draft of this book even before the editing and proofreading exercise started.

The clarity and the ability of the author to inspire us to understand what the reality is away from our imagination is entirely made known and clear from the very moment the conversation opens in the first pages.

Beards Don't Grow in Heaven is an audacious attempt by the author to tell his story in a way that is less travelled by authors of modern writing, this road less travelled is the subject of embarking upon the realm of storytelling with the audience in mind, this reality is not new but it's understandably tasking and makes sense when seen from the standpoint of creative writing.

When I read the early draft of the book "Beards Don't Grow in Heaven, I felt like a battle was raging within me, a battle within but without which it would be nearly impossible to understand the importance of embarking upon this story like a journey which two people were designed to make, with the writer in mind.

The sensitive worldview of children in the society, understandably, is the fact that children are almost not always taken into account in creative circumstances, not particularly because it doesn't hold waters or that their knowledge or views are veiled in images imaginable, I have a singular sense that it is more so because we haven't seen the need as writers of modern literature to mirror in mind the need to view certain realities of the world in the lenses of children, that said, this new part less travelled, but today used by the author is a significant new role in the effort to consider how all voices and experiences are documented in modern civilization.

I haven't seen the end yet of this writer of great promise, what I have established at this new stage is that there is something intense and utterly compelling about his actions in writing, especially his creative use of thoughts, actions, active knowledge and engaged conversations in communicating his ideas and opinions.

One is led to believe that there is more where this came from, in the honest belief that his creative best is yet to be addressed.

The book "Beards Don't Grow in Heaven" while not a fictional book recreates elegance and elemental senses of modern art in ways that holistically takes the reader through a dimension in reality away from the lines reproduced in the pages, through the dirt patched streets and pavements of modern Nigeria, the ancient world of modern Northern Nigeria, the ancient traditions, belief-system, the role of religion, supernatural or superstitious contradictions of human consciousness, these accounts of his bestows upon his audience an untold wealth of avenue through which one makes sense of the world he grew up in and the modernist family he grew into as a young man, the experiences are veiled in a way that that level of innocence allows us as children to interact and interpret the things we are expectedly exposed to as minds in formation.

This is a wonderful recollection of events from the viewpoint of the mind, encircling a lot of different things at different times and places, a world where things are happening in ways that the individual mindset may find intriguing, but with the benefit of hindsight, this new revelation takes us through, leading us as tourists on a mission to enquire and discern, what is the new context to which a world governed by natural laws are allocated with the resources to inspire humanity to action.

I have read a lot of works by many new minds, but this interesting book comes with itself a bright note from which anyone who reads from it will find an alternative route to seeing for themselves that there is something else about the world that a sneak peek won't find.

It is my ultimate goal that this work gets into the hands of as many who are like us on a journey to seek and find, the geographical context of the seekers not necessarily the issue, for those who seek to merit an understanding of the thoughts of humanity must prevail in essence, tracing all aspects of life in the ruins and abandoned routes and tracts forever covered in the dust of history.

Here is my own judgment, it is now in the hands of the enduring seeker to ascertain as to what extent the meanings drawn here by the author are held admissible in light of the questions and answers hiding in the lines and pages of this conversation.

Chì NDù ÈfóGò, Storyteller & Author, *Love in the Eyes of a Widow* & *Oh Son of Dust.*

Port Harcourt, Nigeria.

March 24th, 2021.

CHAPTER

1

THE BUTTERFLY GENERATION

"If children grew up according to early indications, we should have nothing but geniuses." **-Johann Wolfgang von Goethe**

The butterfly, features frequently in ancient times and they are held in high admiration for their beauty and colourful wings. Through their grace, they secured a sacred place in ancient Egyptian art. To this day, a swarm of these beautiful insects flying across flower fields is a precious sight to behold every now and then. The simple act of watching this natural magic can transform us all: Just like it did me. It is an experience that I wish everyone can have at least once in a lifetime. Tourists, naturalists, and curious folks travel thousands of kilometres annually to visit sites with swarms of butterflies and to have this unique experience in different parts of the world where this phenomenon take place. It is an experience that cannot be expressed in the modest words of human language.

Butterflies, because of their nature; their calmness and beauty; signify freedom, creativity and peace. Butterflies also signify more than all these. They are like a natural blueprint of human development. A perfect realistic prototype. A complete one. No other model comes to mind when I am asked questions about the human condition.

The butterfly provides the best model yet in a very optimistic perspective of our progress on the planet as humans. Just like the butterflies, our own lives are also metamorphic, and childhood is the most crucial stage in our transformation. My curiosity about butterflies was first aroused when I was about five years old. I noticed pinned collections of the most beautiful butterflies in a picture frame-a practice of preserving and mounting butterflies on boards which kept them in all their radiant glory except that their lives were cut short. My Dad used to pin dead butterflies at that time to frames. They had the most beautiful patterns, and you would think they were alive. I became fascinated with them and would attempt to catch anyone I see flying around our garden. I even stayed late at night just to trap moths attracted to the candles which lit our living room. I had mistaken them for butterflies at that age until I got a lesson from my father about the difference between these two different species of insects. Butterflies remain one of the most fascinating creatures in nature to me.

By the time you understand the true meaning of childhood, it is usually already too late. It is like a charming house that one lives in and eventually outgrows the doors and the windows; the only way to get back into it might be to pull the roof apart. Will it remain the same house even after all the hassle? Absolutely Not.

It could be the most painful, but yet the most beautiful experience one can ever have. The reality that childhood is over. Thus, the only remedy is that we help children who are still in the process of coming out of this 'house' to be able to enjoy what they see by the time they leave childhood and become adults. What I have just described is a pretty way of saying that once the sanctity of childhood is breached with corruption in any form, it becomes a herculean task for the society to fix the adult the child would become.

However, on the other side of the coin, Pulitzer Prize-winning poet Edna St Vincent Millay says: "Childhood is not from birth to a certain age, and at a certain age, the child grows and puts away childish things. Childhood is the kingdom where nobody dies. Nobody that matters that is." We are given a precious opportunity to go through life once. One of the stages of life that is treasured, irreplaceable and sacrosanct; is childhood. It is the period of life that lasts from birth to adulthood. For many children in Africa, it is the most horrible stage of life.

This is because the African child is confronted by numerous heinous obstacles that challenge the very existence of these precious gifts to humanity. This is not because children in other parts of the world do not face the same or even worse challenges; it is just the way it is.

That often-cherished human experience called childhood is a refuge, a safe zone necessary for the mind to develop properly.

When he is an adult, this ensures that the child can perform optimally, proffering solutions to the inevitable plagues and challenges in his generation. This is the ultimate chance to learn to tackle one's environment and make it work to an advantage for the greater good of all.

Thus, childhood must be protected, because of its importance to the survival of mankind. Children must be protected from the ills that have stained many of us. To cope with these 'stains,' many folks fail and repeat the cycle of hurt and betrayal once again. If we cannot stop this cycle, we should be able to dampen its effects. There will be quagmire generations if we do not do that; generations which are completely lost in the conundrum.

If we can win the hearts of children, we can conquer the world. We could have a butterfly generation. Jean Jacques Rousseau, one of the finest French philosophers of his time, in his book, Émile ou de l'éducation, pleaded: "Why rob these innocents of the joys which pass so quickly." Why can't all children have a beautiful, unforgettable childhood? Why can't childhood be free from polio, wars, and modern-day slavery in Africa and the world? These are the questions we must ask ourselves if we want to create a better world for generations to come. Does it seem like a far-fetched dream? Well, you and I can determine this. We choose, now, at this moment, through our actions, decisions and policies, the kind of childhood experiences our potential butterfly generation in Africa would have. This would be a sneak peek view of the new African child.

The birth of a new Africa can only come through this means. The life stages for Africa's children should be that of a period of joy, wonder, discovery, happiness, play, learning, exploration, and knowledge acquisition about their environment. It should be free of worry and intrusive adult interference. It should also be a period when a child is taught the responsibilities of adulthood.

It is a fact that adults view childhood on a second thought with feelings of nostalgia, joy, and longing for a second experience of it. That is why the fictional character Peter Pan (the boy who wouldn't grow up) which is the story of a boy's eternal childhood that never ends was popular with adults when it was released. It was created by the Scottish novelist James M. Barrie (1860–1937) and it sold about seven million copies in home videos according to the Los Angeles Times in 1991, and the movie won a lot of awards. Once the sanctity of childhood is breached, it becomes a herculean task to fix the adult this child would become. For this reason, Frederick Douglass uttered these words "it is easier to build strong children than to repair broken adults". As we go through the stages of life from being toddlers down to when we become fully grown adults, most of us have observed that one thing has been constant, which is learning.

Whether it is learning to achieve a significant developmental milestone, like walking for the first time, or tackling responsibilities, and learning interesting things about this universe, we keep on learning. Having observed caterpillars, it is difficult to believe that they would one day turn into the beautiful lepidopterans they would become later. They look unsophisticated and ugly. They Crawl around munching every green thing in sight and seem to have no particular purpose. However, the day arrives when they transcend to the pupal stage where they seem to be the archetype of meaningless existence.

They remain in this stage until the day that their final transcendence occurs. One wing after another, the butterfly exits the cocoon and spreads its beautifully patterned wings and flies away. Its beauty and potential, compares to nothing like the ugly caterpillar it once was. Beyond the awesome look, the economic potential of nectar sucking butterflies in cross-pollination and largely in the whole process of how many foods end up on our tables. African children are like these ugly butterfly caterpillars, looking for the right places to transform into wonderful citizens and contribute to global development. The importance of childhood cannot be overstated.

In the early years of development, the emphasis of any reasonable family and society should be to ensure that children learn as much as possible about life and have an enormous amount of fun. They should be taught how to take charge of their thinking and by doing so, become more creative. This helps children to develop into well-rounded adults. The natural curiosity associated with childhood is known to almost all of us.

Every child is curious about life, other children and adults. Children ask questions; they try to put everything into their mouth, poke holes in the ground, fall off small elevations, all in a bid to understand their internal and external loci. Every parent and professional social worker who have observed the early years of a child's development will agree to have witnessed the significant leaps in learning made by children as they grow in their inquisitiveness. These early years are taken seriously in many parts of Europe, America, and certain parts of Africa as we would see in later chapters. A long time ago, in the coastal town of Calabar in West Africa, there lived a legend among the local Efik speaking people whose strong belief in witchcraft and Spiritism had caused so much pain and despair in children's lives.

This pain was fostered on all through complicated customs based on their false and unforgivable naive beliefs. One of these naïve practices; was the murder of twin babies. In their days, the ancient Efik speaking tribes believed that whenever a woman gave birth to twins, it was an evil omen.

Their belief was that one of the babies was 'fathered' by the devil himself. The elders would then murder both babies by strangling them or allowing them to starve to death or they throw them into thick forests for the poor helpless children to be eaten by wild animals in the 'evil' forest, since no one could tell which of them was fathered by the devil according to their erroneous belief. The mother was also shunned by the society for having had sexual dealings with Satan. It was the arrival of a woman named, Mary Slessor, a passionate Scottish missionary to Nigeria who came to be warmly called 'The

White Queen of Calabar' in the late 19th century that put an end to this heinous act. She adopted many twin babies who were thrown out to die and she prevented many more deaths by speaking out bravely against the barbaric practice. Mary did not have a smooth, sailing childhood. She was raised by an alcoholic father and a God-fearing mother. Her father's habit put the family in a precarious financial situation.

Mary was forced to start working at eleven to support the family being the second of seven children. She soon became the breadwinner of the family. It was at this age that she learnt the noble practice of altruism. It was also at this stage that her dream to do philanthropic work in Africa began. She became a Christian at an early age and would always be found reading her bible and any other book she could find. On August 5, 1876, Mary sailed from Liverpool for Calabar in Southern Nigeria. She was twenty-seven years old at the time. Not long after her ship docked, the arduous task she had chosen dawned on her.

There were so many challenges in this strange West African country. Alligators were swimming all around and also basking under the sun on the riverbanks. After seeing many strange practices such as having to dip one's hand in boiling hot oil to prove the innocence of an alleged accusations, she experienced a culture shock. In some situations, wives and slaves were buried with their dead husbands to 'escort' him into the spirit world. It was all too much for her to bear. She decided to be brave and she began to study the local language; Efik and she mastered the language within a short period. She also learnt many things about the culture of the Calabar people.

This set her in place for the great things she is fondly remembered for in the world today. Particularly touching to her was the custom of twin infanticide. Using her newly acquired skill and training as a Christian, she set about negotiating and challenging the practice of the killing of twins by the Efik people.

Though she often came down with diarrhea, malaria, and other tropical diseases, she continued her mission for close to forty years until she died on January 13, 1915, at sixty-six. Until her death, she had saved hundreds of twins thrown into the forest and left to die. And her efforts in saving these little children's lives proved successful with the acceptance of twins by the Efik people and all over Africa as Gifts from God rather than cursed beings. Her story is being told around the world today. Many twins in Nigeria today owe their lives to this great show of altruism and humanness by her. They are in the butterfly generation.

CHAPTER

2

LOOKING BEYOND RELIGION'S IRON CURTAIN

"Allow children to be happy in their own way, for what better way will they ever find" **-Gandhi**

We all assume that children need to be taught and shown the way. I do not believe that this is the best route. Though it may have been the norm for many years in different civilizations, we now live in a new aeon. Education should show children how to look introspectively and find out who they are and who they can become. At what point does the problem of religious self-ostracism occur? In my early days, there was no virtual veil that separated us from each other. I speak here of my friends who come from families who hold beliefs that were alien to us. For many years as children, these veils had not yet been created in the minds of the would-be adults. It was simple. We saw our friends for who they were.

Their character was as clear as crystal. No one had yet hidden behind the curtain. We knew that certain behaviours were socially unacceptable. We tried to tight-ropewalk our way through the maze of social responsibility at that level.

It is true that on a larger scale, it is a more serious affair. However, it is not enough reason to vent animosity towards our fellow humans, most especially with the friends we have had a fair, harmonious coexistence with from our childhood. Why can't the harmonious coexistence we enjoyed as children be replicated in adulthood?

This is the paradox that still troubles me and of course many people who share this line of thought. I still remember with vivid clarity how easy it was resolving conflict among my peers without sieving it through partial views. Without using a periscope polished with nepotism and religious bias to view issues. Without playing that card, it was easy to settle the odd boy who used the money meant to buy a football for chewing gums, lollipops and sweets instead. Those inborn conflict resolution skills sunk in as we sailed towards our individual and collective monochromic religious ports. A man's race or religion should not be the crux of the matter when we have to engage each other.

It would definitely be a success when we raise an African generation of children ignorant of the prejudices that taint the adulthood of dysfunctional grown children and make them use public labels such as religious affiliation or tribal leanings in their day-to-day activities and interactions with the human race. These should not be the basis for decision making in any democratic society. Not for an individual and definitely not for the public.

Not even at this stage of our growing democracy and of course, never. Decisions made on such preconditions only create malfunctioning cogs in the democratic wheel that has long since escaped inertia and settled on the African continent. It is easy to think that children are lost in their world to the logical mind; thus, must be shown the way. Most times, this is not true. We do not lead children to the light. Children come with the light. Every child comes into the world equipped with their own lamps. Perhaps, it is in how to keep their lamps oiled that we must show and direct children; not with words but in the manner in which our rusted lamps have continued to hold oil and light our paths and the paths of others in the hazy journey of life.

If the world must witness significant progress and development, children must be told the absolute truth. That no monsters are lurking in the closets, no gods, or angels above nor demons below. We must let them know that they are the only hope this planet, humans and other forms of life on earth might have. It is apparent that the superfluous fables created by ancient men have provided the fuel on which many needless wars have been kindled and to which the tune of politics plays.

Since all children start by questioning the world around them, what does it serve to feed their neurons with well-cooked lies? The beauty of life is in it objectively unravelling its secrets. This is the only way humans have made progress from humid caves to the urban settlements around the world today. And we have done beyond that. We continue to discover the vastness of our universe every day. Keeping any child who asks questions in the dark is dangerous for the future.

While philosophy might illuminate the mind and provide the means to internal freedom, religion has kept humanity at a standstill. This endangers our survival in the cosmos. It is science that can create any more opportunities for communal growth and global development and this will secure our small planet's future in a vast and pernicious universe. We cannot leave these things to chance.

I personally think that when as a child you are first told of the hell hoax by a priest, the wisest action is to reserve your ticket immediately because its price rises astronomically as time goes on. Indoctrinating a child is setting him on a path we think is best for them. Even when done with the best intentions, this does not always lead to a happy life as promised.

Most humans spend a tremendous amount of time fighting the tendencies to do what they were told to do and doing precisely the opposite of what they were instructed not to do. Such human potential when the capacity of the neurological system is considered is wasted needlessly in multiple neural pathways that serve no use. For many, religion serves like a dinghy to cross from one side of a river to another, but it would not be sufficient. Once on this other side of intellectual freedom and autonomy, you no longer need this dinghy. Why don't we teach children to build their boats by themselves instead of feeding off their naivety and telling them creative lies?

One of the many terrible things about religion is that it treats humans as vile savages that need to be tamed by beliefs to 'force' conditioned well- being. On the contrary, humans are capable of exceeding the religious, moral threshold if they are given a chance and without the taint of conditioning.

Like the great Pavlov trained his dogs to respond to auditory stimulus synchronised with their mealtimes by ringing a bell before feeding them, it is the same way many humans are educated to think in a certain way. And like for his dogs, whose sensory stimuli of smell and hearing was limited to the tinkering sound of brass, so are some humans limited. What a pity! The hatching of eggs, for example, looks challenging from a biological standpoint.

The chick's muscles are weak, but the shell must crack to be genuinely called birds. Empathy might lead you to crack open the eggshell. Still, as is often the case, most of such chicks that are aided artificially to crack their shells do not survive nature's elements. This is because they lose the chance to build the strength necessary to overcome their shell's safety and in order to confront the world, which is a fundamental process needed to ignite their capacity to thrive. This is sadly lost to itchy hands.

This is the same as the human condition. No child is born with a natural inclination for evil. The human conscience is undoubtedly there for a purpose: as a guide. It is as useful as the limbs. Like a torch burning through the dark paths of life, it leads us through this beautiful maze. But as with any human component, disuse results in atrophy. Have the adults who flaunt around with pride of having 'raised morale' kids under various guises succeeded in leading themselves first? With their atrophied consciences, they teach that a moral compass is within the pages of a religious book. How hilarious! A book? Compared to the depth of the human conscience? Generations of humans have been led ignorantly over the cliff.

It seems repulsive that a moral threshold is set inevitably and unconsciously by these ancient methods. We live in a better world today, not because of messages from the past left as clues, neither from those left in the Hohlenstein-Stadel cave in the Swabian Jura in Germany thirty-five to forty thousand years ago to the heap of religious texts we have today, there are no morals that can be gleaned from them that a child with a clean mind cannot discover.

For children, the best we could ever do as adults would be to guide them; to light their candles so they would lead the way ahead of us. Isn't that why they are children? Their world should sparkle more brightly than ours because their dilemmas would be different. Through living, let us leave the past behind so that a new and beautiful world which would require malleable humans liberated from a brittle and atrophied conscience would be realized. Religion is crying wolf where there is none.

Indoctrination is not only about religion. It is the act of considering children as pawns and minions in whatever whimsical pursuits we want to accomplish in life. It is unnerving to think this is the reality around many parts of the world. People can indoctrinate their children into certain professions to fulfil their wishes and aims. Such selfish goals have even involved gruesome paths like terrorism.

My assertion is not that children should be wholly denied religious instruction. However, I condemn entirely religion being taught to kids as an objective view and method to navigate the world when the texts on which they are based are nothing less than surrealist fiction meant for an epoch that we have long crossed.

Every child looks towards the future, but religion only serves as a cog in the wheel of progress uniquely for those willing to move us all to a higher echelon of existence. For instance, to understand medicine and law, a good knowledge of Greek and Roman Polytheology helps immensely because medical students learn of Pandora's box, Hygeaia and Aesculapius the universal symbol for the medical profession.

As for religious texts that have ridden on humanity's longing for hope to be one of the most successful literary works, children must read these books as literary works and nothing more because that is precisely what they are. How else would an adult understand the idiomatic expression, 'fleecing the sheep' without a thorough knowledge of the bible? In today's world, we cannot continue to decry the pitiable state that religion has led certain individuals and societies to bring shame and disgust to the otherwise dignified human race. Terrorists inspired by religious texts, millions of preventable deaths occurring every minute because supposedly educated individuals in the West and Central parts of Africa recognize the church as an emergency centre where they rush an individual suffering a cardiac arrest to, instead of strategically located hospitals.

In May 2018, three patients receiving treatment for the Ebola virus disease that reached epidemic proportions in the west and central Africa in 2014 were taken to a church for healing prayers from a treatment centre run by the international Non-governmental organization: Medecins Sans Frontières (Doctors Without Borders) in Mbandaka, Democratic Republic of Congo.

Their families appeared with motorbikes and virtually escaped with them from the centre and took them to church. Two of the patients sadly died, and the third was returned to the medical centre. Ignorant actions like these are quite common on the African continent where superstition reigns supreme under the guise of religious illumination. The government cannot help such societies overcome this ignorance until individuals choose to use the libraries and hospitals near their dwelling places rather than losing sleep praying over a corpse until the ubiquitous work of natural microbes makes it unbearable and the body is moved to the morgue. For how long can we tolerate such dangerous ideologies? I have shared with my close friends that if I ever have a cardiac arrest, I hope to be in the right environment and not surrounded by a bunch of ignorant raga muffins.

We even have to deal with the problems where births are taken in churches with hands blessed with ferocious microbes that would have made Ignaz Semmelweis really wield a whip at these self-appointed know-it-all folks. If children are allowed to question the world, many more discoveries would be made about our natural world that will add meaning to our place in the universe and make our living experience more fulfilling, enjoyable, and maybe honourable.

It seems to me that there is a high association between the accusations of childhood witchcraft and several antisocial behaviours by adults later in life. The same names would crossmatch undoubtedly if a study is performed by psychologists. The practice of accusing children of witchcraft is common in many parts of West and Central Africa such as Nigeria, Senegal, and the Democratic Republic of Congo.

These victims of witchcraft abuse are not called the same names in all of Africa. In the Congo, they are Ndoki. In Tanzania, they are labelled 'djinn'. The Yorubas in Nigeria call them Aje, the Igbos call them Ogbanjé in the same country, while in Rwanda they are called Abazimu. This is an area that needs an in-depth study by sociologists to address this problem from its root.

I look back with a regretful nostalgic feeling at the number of friends and acquaintances affected by this practice and accused of being a witch in our society. Today, it feels like I had lived in a European 17th century partial civilization when witches were burnt at stake. When I read historical texts written by European authors debunking this practice, I felt like I have crossed two different timelines having witnessed such myself as a child and seeing that this way of life was accepted by the society I lived in without batting an eyelid.

The fact seems to be that these accusations were a simple case of naming and hanging a 'bouc d'emmisaire' for seemingly unsolvable problems in the family or community. Such children are usually psychologically defeated by the time they become adults due to the abuse and neglect they suffered as children as a result of the label they carried growing up. They often become victims of rape, murder, and prolonged starvation. I witnessed the maltreatment three sons meted to their mother, when she was accused of witchcraft, supposedly the cause of lack of progress and stagnation in the family. Before my eyes, it was a repeat of the Salem witch hunt trials in the United States in the late 17th century.

Like in the US, the maxim of this woman's children was 'suffer not a witch to live' which they obviously cherry-picked from their bible. In their witlessness, they accused their mother of morbid witchcraft and the cause of financial stagnation in the family, rather than looking at the economic depression we were all undergoing as a nation under General Sani Abacha's dictatorship who was the Nigerian leader between 1993 and 1998. I remember seeing them drag their mother on the tarred road in the streets of Kuru, in North Central Nigeria, until she was bleeding profusely from her peeling skin. Her head was bashed in by clubs and rocks.

They finally led her to the cemetery where they killed her brutally. Although they were adults, her sons may have been raised in a culture where they believe in the existence and esoteric witchcraft world, which unfortunately led them to think that their mother was a witch. Such summary and barbaric executions are carried out in ignoble delusions. When victims are not killed but tortured, the survivors of such stigma live in fear and may develop complicated mental health problems. They often accept the verdict that has been decreed over their lives by their families and society.

Some of them really begin to think that maybe they are really a witch and are missing something about leading a normal life. They find it difficult to reintegrate into the society and build trust with their peers due to fear of fresh accusations and persecution. Their horror and pain know no bounds. Sometimes, and to their detriment, the same society goes further to declare them irredeemable lunatics. Such malformation in the grandeur of Africa's beautiful community, potentially should be traced to its source and excised just like a surgeon skilfully assaults cancerous tumour. This must be done most subtly. The dark days of such accusations are not entirely over in Africa, even though there is no reason why such savagery should continue.

In January 2016, a Danish woman living in Africa had an astounding encounter in Nigeria when she bumped into a young toddler abandoned by his family in the middle of nowhere riddled with worms and emaciated from starvation and outright neglect by his kinsmen. My friends in Paris drew my attention to this case after stunning pictures of Ms Anja Ringgren Loven rode on the waves of the internet and social media where she was pictured giving him water to drink from a water bottle. Hope as he came to be called was taken to the hospital by this kind Danish woman, an aid worker, for treatment where he received attention for his worms and malnutrition. He also had to receive daily blood transfusions to balance his red blood cells, depleted overtime during his peril.

There was a global sympathy to his condition which resulted in a movement that raised about $1 million to meet his needs. When I heard about the international efforts of many around the world towards the ordeal of just one child, I was first of all impressed by the sheer generosity of people around the world to someone they would probably never meet, but at the same time, I wondered why the world had let down many other children to perish, particularly in Africa.

Many activists toil night and day to bring this to the attention of people around the world who may be able to rewrite the narrative of the lives of thousands of children who are victims of childhood witchcraft abuse and potentially a million more who may be under threat of such savage violence. Indeed, if the local and international community had lent a listening ear to Hope's situation, it can also lobby politicians so that policies and laws are not only passed to protect children from witchcraft abuse but ensure that they have a quality life that is above the minimum standards. And comparable to that in most prosperous countries of the world. I am happy for Hope, and I am equally excited for the thousands of children who are being spared such a disastrous start in life due to the good work of many formidable activists and AID workers like Ms Loven. Hope is one lucky child, but we cannot always count on mere chance in such a dangerous world. We must continue to charge forward and create a marvellous wonderland for children no matter what part of the world they are born in.

Our natural inclination as humans is to live as free beings, free to explore the length and breadth of the earth and possibly the universe's whole extent. We abhor everything that keeps us captive and deprives us of the freedom to express our independent personality, which is unique and different from everyone in the communities we find ourselves in. Any opposition to this is asphyxiating and results in rebellions between humans which results in creating dysfunctional societies. Many humans try to live as freely as possible despite the tendencies of despotic governments to restrict them or even the illusionary freedom provided by capitalism. People are also limited by family, and the luxury of being born into various conditions they think are inimical to their liberty and the ultimate expression of their human experience. Most times, people do all they can to regain the freedom taken from them by the statistical law of nature by making great sacrifices and some of them succeed. One of such people who went to such a great length to explore the realms of godlike freedom was Siddhartha, who is better known by the name Gautama Buddha or simply as 'The Buddha'.

Siddhartha was born in the present-day Nepal, in a region known as Lumbini to a wealthy royal family. His name Siddhartha means 'the one who achieves his aim'. He was born into opulence as a prince who had everything that he could wish for at his disposal. Servants and maids were at his disposal right from birth to attend to his minutest whim and displeasure, his mother died during childbirth.

Although Siddhartha had a perfect start at life; spoilt to the hilt with all he could wish for, he found out that he was not happy with the situation of his inner and outer world. Prashant, a friend, who is from the present-day location of the village where Buddha is said to have been born, described to me how it was during the lifetime of Siddhartha before he came to be known as the Buddha. Prashant and I first met when I arrived in Paris for my master's degree in the summer of 2014.

In fact, on my arrival, I had nowhere to pass the night because my visa and other travel arrangements from Nigeria came at the very last minute. I had little time to pick a few precious belongings before boarding the next flight to this city of lights and love. Exhausted from my flight, I still could make it to lectures on the same day at the university to catch up on the backlog of work I had. That evening, Prashant kindly offered that I stay at his place for the night until I sorted out my accommodation.

He treated me to the best chicken curry I ever ate from his part of Asia, and we washed it down with French red wine. Over dinner, I realized that he was the first Nepali I was meeting, and the discussion soon veered from first time pleasantries to regional politics, and I started a philosophical inquest about life in Nepal and how their worldview was entirely different from the classical Western thought. I got a long lecture from my new friend. Over the next two years, we would have similar evenings where Prashant would make his famous curry and invite me over for dinner, drinks, and talks. I learned a lot about Nepal but also about Buddhism in an exceptionally very practical way. My planned trip to Nepal to visit Siddhartha's birthplace with my friend was botched due to some unforeseen reasons, but Prashant made it home alone to visit his family and returned with a medium-sized burnt clay statuette of Buddha himself which he gifted to me.

To continue our story, fearing that his soul will be contaminated with evil and sadness, Siddhartha's father and other palace officials did everything in their power to prevent the young man from witnessing the state of the palace's subjects who were mostly living in deplorable state of poverty. Fortunately, one day, Siddhartha saw first-hand the life outside the court, and he came to terms with the anguish the people were undergoing.

He decided to estrange himself from a life of magnificence by escaping the palace life even though he was married to a loving wife and had a beautiful child, to pursue a path of spiritual growth and awakening. He was simply convinced that there was more to life than the typical day to day hassle. For many years, he would travel discreetly in the humblest way with the poorest of the poorest in his quest for knowledge and enlightenment. Luck shone on him when he finally achieved nirvana and claimed to yet be in touch with the deepest recesses of his mind and spirit-this happens to be the ultimate goal of Buddhists the world over today. In other words, he achieved transcendence, and his words continue to teach wisdom to millions around the world today. An unsettling pinch led him out of his golden cage into the freedom that earned him his name and gave him a place under the skies.

As an African, I can relate to the Buddha's quest for simplicity and not for a life of excessive extravagant comfort and unworthy opulence. The point where the story of Buddha unfolds is the beginning of the story of every Almajiri child on the streets of West-Africa. The pursuit of freedom and knowledge of self; freedom from want, freedom from the oppression of the mind and body. Unfortunately, many end up in unbreakable chains.

I have perceived that in the original ideals of what is called the Almajiri system in Northern Nigeria. However, this system has developed an aggressive tumour that has corrupted and truncated the dreams of millions of children into unamendable pieces and shards. Most times, for a child, it is a dream lost and never to be found. For a family, it is a bundle of love thrown away in the abyss. For society, it is a call to live with monsters and potential dysfunctional humans. This is the loss of the Almajiri system. This same longing for purpose and recognition under the stars that inspired the Buddha may be what ignited the hideous Almajiri wave that has enslaved many rather than enabling them to discover who they are, from the inside, and how to glide on their own wings rather than perish under the clasp of another human's grip. But who is an Almajiri? Let's tease it out in the next chapter.

CHAPTER

3

THE ALMAJIRI-TRAPPED BEHIND RELIGION'S IRON CURTAIN

---

*"From my tender stage of life, I was treated like I have no rights. And towards the future I cannot rise."- **Iblajo***

The Almajiri system is designed to teach pupils self-sustenance and virtues of life, such as honesty and faith in God. It is similar to the Shaolin temple practice which is widespread in China and many parts of Asia but predominant in China. Almaijiranci is a system that aims to equip Muslim children, with the spiritual knowledge of self and Allah at no cost. It is a lifelong training system intended to take the disciple from a mere child to the level of a scholar in Islamic studies and in the Arabic language. It is quite an interesting educational system which is very different from the western education system. Students are taught to fend for themselves and 'pay' their 'mallam' or teacher about $1 a week from the proceeds of their begging and other forms of work they engage in to raise money.

A mallam is usually an adult male caretaker who is well-schooled in Quranic teachings, Arabic and the Islamic way of life or conduct. The role of such mallam is to ensure that these children perform the five daily Islamic prayers while also teaching them about the Quran, Arabic language and all the open secrets.

All these are aimed for the child to live a fulfilled life as a faithful Muslim who is willing to defend his faith at all costs in the face of tyranny or persecution. The teaching style can be quite coercive as the mallams usually hold a horsewhip which they easily swing at will to drive home a point and to ensure that the lessons are followed with full attention. It is not uncommon to find these children with scarred tissue on their skins. The reputation of these mallams have been tainted by a large number of cases of abuse levied against them. Many of such stories are true, but some of these descriptions have not been spared by popular hyperbolic imageries. This does not help in the proper formation of Almajiri friendly policies through a purely rational pattern.

There is a structured calendar where the disciples are allowed to go home in an informal holiday to visit their parents and siblings who may have graduated from the system. The mallam is not paid formally by the students, but they contribute to his well-being by working on his farmland or other establishments he may own as a way of giving back in exchange for the knowledge they have gained.

After their short holiday, most pupils are not willing to go back to continue this process due to the harsh life they have endured. Many of them are unable to go on holidays since they cannot afford the cost of transportation. These ones stay on in a foreign land for extended periods. Some of these lucky ones start up small scale businesses to support themselves and abandon the system altogether. Many Nigerian citizens, including those who oppose their presence, patronize them (Almajiri children). It is estimated that over 80% of households utilize the services of Almajiri children either occasionally or permanently in Sokoto State (located in North-Western, Nigeria) alone.[1] But for the rest of them, they are not able to escape the life of begging that was hoisted upon them even though soliciting for alms and living off charity is forbidden in Islam with the exception of people who are invalid or disabled.

Although the system was not initially designed to put them through these unbearable conditions, they were left with no choice due to neglect from their families and the society who treat them like a pariah. Common chores in the life of an Almajiri boy in its jolly days included washing dishes, preparing meals for 'foster' families, and going on errands to the market to name a few. They were basically handymen for any lowly task that needed to be done, but their condition was still bearable at the time.

The same way a Shaolin Monk embarks on a journey of self-discovery; so, the Almajiri system was also initially designed at least in principle. How is it then that the rivers have over-flown their banks in our day? Is it a simple case of abdication of responsibilities on our part? How has this system become an eyesore to the 'civilized' eyes? It is my thinking; that many of the survivors of this kind of educational system who have been able to glide through several echelons in the social ladder, would not dare to admit their childhood experiences. Whether it was a good or bad experience; and how this system of education has affected their lives, we don't hear testimonies about this educational system, except behind closed doors. I believe that their stories, however, would rekindle the candle in many hearts in Nigeria and in other parts of West Africa where this system is still in practice. This is because it is only when we share these stories that we can get a global understanding of the cards on the table, and then we can know how to decipher what is on in the labyrinth.

Dogs are man's best friends, but African sages have it written on tablets of stone; that one should not call on a dog with a whip in hand. Almajiri is based on the reward system, in this case, eternal rewards. The Almajiri system can be traced back as far as the eleventh century A.D in West Africa, and its debut is quite indistinguishable from the arrival of Islam on the sub-continent.

One of the prevalent misconceptions about this educational system today is that these Muslim parents have a brood of kids they cannot cater for and resort to sending them out to fend for themselves. In reality, most of their parents can care for their needs, but they place great importance on their kids' religious indoctrination. Therefore, many parents vow that their children must complete the Almajiri education system before they commence the formal western education.

Due to their early separation from their parents (many leave home as early as six years old), millions of them do not develop properly emotionally due to the long family separation, and this mental deficit can prolong even into adulthood. Every year, millions of Almajiri children miss their routine vaccinations due to the educational system's nomadic nature and they end up with preventable diseases like poliomyelitis, varicella, measles, and other vaccine-preventable infections.

However, the untold story is the number of them who survive due to 'natural immunisation' from exposure to diseases and thus perpetuate the idea that they do not need to be immunized against infections. In a bid to survive against all odds, many of these children in their quest for enlightenment are invariably cut off from the kindness of the society, resort to eating spoilt food almost all the time as well as sleep in unimaginable conditions on pieces of carton unshielded in any form whatsoever from the drastically dropping night temperatures in cities like Kano, Jos, and Sokoto in Nigeria in poorly ventilated, overcrowded, and unhygienic milieus.

Like a Shaolin prodigy in the far East-Shanghai, China, the Nigerian Almajiri pupil is armed with his bowl each morning and a strong heart guided by faith to storm the streets every single day of his life. This arduous task will require every inch of his sinews to be in action and every mental toughness he can glean in his possession to serve him.

He requires muscular strength to cope with his uncharted nomadic roving and mental tenacity to cope with the multiple rejections and abuses he will receive from his fellow citizens, and the physical and verbal attacks inflicted on him daily. The life skills he gets from this kind of Spartan lifestyle is supposed to transform him into a finely refined adult if he survives the trials he faces in the decade long training until he becomes a youth.

For the Islamic migrant pupil, it has usually been challenging to garner help beyond mere concern and pity because of the prevailing thoughts that the Almajiri child's rewards are priceless spiritual gains that are in no way comparable to the ephemeral pleasures and possessions of worldly life. People who see nothing wrong in these children leading a life of destitution have often used the above line of reasoning in defending this humiliating practice. With this line of thinking, it becomes challenging to convince them that the Almajiri really 'suffers' any discomfort at all since such Islamic knowledge is explicitly desired and encouraged to be highly sought for by devoted Muslims.

Proponents of this system also decry the non-absorption of these street children by formal western education centres. They believe that the children and their parents have no other option than subjecting them to this form of non-conventional training and instruction.

Africa is replete with hordes of children on the streets, and this problem is not necessarily unique to Nigeria or West Africa. Whether we are discussing the shegues of Congo-Kinshasa, the talibes of Senegal and Egypt, the faseurs of Congo-Brazaville, the tsotsis of South of Africa, or the Almajirai of Nigeria, one thing is common: they are all just children trying to survive the harsh demands of nature to satisfy their primary physiological needs. Among these children, only the talibes of Senegal and the Almajirai in Nigeria share a common purpose: the pursuit of Islamic enlightenment and erudition.[2] Much of what is valid for the Almajiri in Nigeria is also very accurate for Senegal's talibes. Ghana, Niger, Cameroun, and other West-African nations all suffer from this phenomenon's plight under various names, but the goal is always the same. However, we choose to see it, these street children contribute to major social problems and they also constitute a tough social group to handle in Africa. I have met these children countless times, but two encounters with this group of children have left an indelible mark in my memory for life.

As far as I can remember, my first real encounter with extraneous poverty and the fact that there were less privileged children than me, (who were at risk), happened at my aunt's wedding, a joyous moment of my life.

During the festivities, I was coming out of the wedding reception, which was held in one of the lecture theatres of the university of Jos in Nigeria. Many years ago, I cannot remember what date it was exactly, but it must have been around 1995. We all came out of the hall to admire the surrounding rocks, nature, and the lawn. While doing so, it turned out that it was at that moment that I saw those desperate eyes piercing into every fibre of my being. Rice is traditionally served at Nigerian weddings, and I had just eaten a portion of this ubiquitous delicacy. I was walking casually with the rest of my rice packed in Styrofoam when I heard a gust of wind rush from behind and a hand grabbed from my hands all that I had.

My pack of rice went in one direction, and my bottle of soft drink went in another direction. For me, it was the funny classical tale of chasing two hares because I was paralysed with fear and undecided on what action to take. This elementary robbery had been carried out by a clan of children who ran straight into me from behind and grabbed my pack of food from which I had only just had a few spoonfuls. I never understood what happened at that age, and I did not know what to do, but instinctively, I started my pursuit in the direction of these juvenile thieves.

I ran after the one who took the pack of rice. I ran until I started gasping for breath. I continued to run with my whole strength even though my chest felt like it would explode from pain. These kids were stronger and swifter than me, but I was not going to give up easily. When I finally caught up with them, I amazingly saw the clan of children more clearly; one of them was dressed in shabby oversized clothes that permitted him to look clean enough to enter the wedding venue. The chase led me to their dwelling place. It was a small enclave in the rock behind the reception venue (like a crevice), but it seemed like a giant cave for children of that size, the place reeked of urine and faeces, and was also littered with refuse, but I spotted a sleeping mat and some neatly arranged water bottles in the corner.

My parents and other family members were unaware of my whereabouts. Everyone was in a full-blown celebratory mood. The kind that comes with Nigerian wedding ceremonies. In the simmered light that sliced lazily into the cave, I saw again, the wildest and scariest eyes staring at me. They looked dangerously bright in the darkness. They stood out in the dark like the glow that a dog's eye gives in poor luminosity.

It was one that spelt hazard and the resolve to do anything to survive. It is not a memory that I like to revisit often. In a swift one motion move, I briskly turned and scuttled away. I was only about 6 years old. I immediately gave up my joy, and a particular weakness and disgust that I cannot explain in words captured my spirit. This day remains engraved in my mind. I had seen the eyes of poverty, and it was the eyes of rage. I do not know if I can call them beastly or lovely eyes, but they had the look of vulnerability, wildness, and a plea for mercy- from me. That was what hurt me the most. Who was I that kids my age would plead as if for their lives when I was not even yet a teenager while at the same time maintaining a dangerous guard of their well-being from invasion by a privileged child? The combination of these emotions was too much for my young mind to bear.

I did not tell my parents where I had been when they were looking for me to take photos with the newlywed since I was also the ring bearer at my Aunt's wedding ceremony. A big chunk of my childhood happiness was dented forever after that event. I would always have nightmares and see those eyes for many years afterwards. What I am sure to have seen in those eyes is everything I have described plus unbridled rage. I began to ask myself many questions until this day, but it was only a typical event that had happened to me. I had made my first official contact with my first group of Almajiri children (Almajirai).

It is no doubt that the Almajiri children are a stick of social dynamite waiting to explode.[2] As stated earlier, because Almajiri children are separated very early from their parents, and may rarely ever see them, they are deprived of basic parental emotions, leading them to lack affection for others. This is even more pronounced in a community where they have to roam, plead with their lives, work, and wait for crumbs that fall of the rich man's table or worse still, scavenge for food in the refuse for livelihood. Many become cold-hearted as they grow but sometimes, the unwavering flame of natural conscience continues to shine through them.

It is not uncommon for them to become tools of catastrophic Armageddon in the hands of politicians and other people in the society who seek cheap but loyal labour to execute their dangerous whims on the public. It is common knowledge in Nigeria that these children are involved in underage voting in the north-eastern parts of Nigeria at the behest of a mallam to vote for a politician of his choice. Suffrage is set at eighteen years in Nigeria, but it is not uncommon to have found that children as young as nine participated in choosing who will lead the country's affairs in complete ignorance of the consequences of their choices.

Investigations have also revealed that most religious crises fought in northern Nigerian states such as Kaduna in the year 2000 and in Jos in 2001 and 2010 had the bloody participation of Almajiri foot soldiers who did so by the instruction of their religious scholars. The hydra-headed insurgency in the north of Nigeria by the Islamic sect Boko Haram teems with Almajiri among its fighters who have found a sense of purpose and brotherhood in their cause. These fighters strongly believe that their slaughtering of an infidel will fling open the gates of paradise to them and grant them a hero's welcome to heaven if they die fighting to spread their extremist Islamic ideologies which they believe is the only justice that the world needs to achieve philosophical equilibrium.

Efforts to put a stop to this system have often been met with strong resistance. The general hostile opposition to any move to ameliorate Almajiri children's condition and end the system has often been misinterpreted as direct attacks on Islam. The first efforts to mitigate this practice in Nigeria dates back to 1959. Parents were sensitized and alerted to the dangers of exposing their children to the streets' unadorned life. This problem has lingered on partly because of the religious value placed on Almajiri scholarship. The question that is left unanswered is 'are we willing to do away with a 'spiritual quest' that is inimical to physical well-being?'

The responsibility of bringing redemption to the children

caught up in this system rests on the shoulders of every one of us! In the tunnel towards the light of life, one either sees a train coming ahead or out of deliberate choice, chooses to see a new panorama unfolding. I prefer the latter. Everyone who sees the light ahead and decides to follow would understand this. On a first coup d'oeil, it looks like a can of worms. But at a second glance, it looks different, maybe like a can of spoilt milk to a starving man.

But on several more glances, one finds that there are a lot of things that could be learnt from kids in such situations. It is a diamond mine. And like every diamond mine, only the polishers can identify and transform a diamond from its rough state. And I can imagine the thoughts on their pure minds after a hot, sweaty day under the Sun, with absolutely nothing for their hungry stomachs. The lucky ones who can have a few alms drop in their plates would attract bigger and stronger bullies. It sends bullies behind their backs. In the real sense of it, it is the game of the huntsman and his game. I choose to say that every kid should be rewarded in his day.

To expedite the end of this shameful system, child begging must be prohibited, and the Islamic teachers and parents should be reoriented and prevented from sending children out to beg. There must be a value system orientation in West African countries affected by this scourge. This change will not happen in the twinkling of an eye, but the earlier we set the ship of change sailing, the sooner society will reap its benefits. To enable a swift transition and for sustainable change to percolate the community, the Almajiri system should be officially recognized and reformed in a way that respects the rights of every child as stipulated in the child's good act ratified by Nigeria and also as enshrined in the United Nations' declaration of human rights.

It would make a tremendous difference if Qur'anic schools could be erected and funded by the state located evenly across these countries' breadth to prevent dangerous underage migration. Many individuals, non-governmental organizations and the government have put a lot of effort into curbing these ills in Nigeria, and they must be commended for their actions. However, we must apply novel methods to address this age-old problem with a different level of thinking when considering children and childhood as you will be able to garner from this book.

Nigeria's former president, Goodluck Jonathan, attempted to reform the Almajiri system in northern Nigeria but his efforts soon faded into oblivion after his government was replaced. This eyesore continues even after him, and his successor President Muhammadu Buhari has said that there is no immediate plan to ban the slavery-like practice- to the disappointment of many concerned parties as you can imagine. The forerunners in the pursuit of a better life for the African child have not let such governmental sleight of hand deter their efforts, and the struggle is on every day across the continent to improve the situation. But it seems that while brave humanitarians try to restore dignity in these children's lives, the problem sprouts more horrendous hydra-heads with fangs ready to bite into the decent progress that has been made.

I arrived in Luzern, Switzerland one rainy evening towards the end of summer in 2019 for studies and I thought of writing parts of this book after I must have rested a little. While I was setting up my writing table, I decided to watch the news online to catch up with things happening back home. What I saw that night on several international news channels making the headlines completely broke my heart once again. Almost 500 boys and men were rescued when Nigerian Police busted an Islamic school in Kaduna State in northern Nigeria after receiving a helpful tip-off. Among the rescued were boys as young as five years old, many of whom had suffered sexual and physical abuse. The photos taken by the Nigerian Police brought back memories of the trans-Atlantic slave trade era. These boys and men were chained to old car wheels, bound in hands, and feet perpetually.

One of the rescued men who was supposed to be in South Africa studying for his master's degree at the time recounted how many young boys were freely sexually abused and were allowed to perform sexual acts among themselves as one of the few behaviours that were not punished. They were hung from the ceiling and tortured mercilessly when they tried to escape. Many of them also came from neighbouring African countries such as Burkina Faso, Mali, and Niger.

They were sent over by their parents to acquire Islamic knowledge in this exceptional Islamic school which was nothing short of a gulag experience. Many of the adults who found themselves there were deceived and lured there by their families or plainly kidnapped. Their crime was that they seemed to have strayed away from the Islamic path. As I realized that many of them had spent several years of their lives in such hideous conditions, I switched off the Television.

I thought about it all through the night and imagined what those children and adults must have frightfully experienced. I considered how their minds might have been scarred. A few days later, I concluded that nothing would be done to the "torture house" if it were a few years ago. While I was having coffee in the morning, my mind began to develop alternate optimistic scenarios.

The anxiety built up in me over the past few days started to subside as I comforted myself with the thought that the Nigerian Police acted in those children and men's best interests. As peace began to return to my mind, I concluded that just maybe, a flame of hope which will soon be blazing exists for the African child after all.

CHAPTER

4

THE BUTCHERS OF THE WORLD~EDUCATION

"Educate yourselves to liberate yourselves AFRICA!"
-Stephen Marley

The impending transformational power of an educated Africa is the eighth wonder of our modern world. It is not something that anyone can ever visualise or completely comprehend. Though, it is possible to perceive it. The misperception seems to be more of a bureaucratic epidemic. This perception has fuelled international organisations' hearts, investing billions of dollars in Africa's future in every form of aid. A model for the new world to come. Unfortunately, this view has eluded us and the minds of many leaders. It is this self-induced short-sightedness that has plagued the African continent. It makes us see the 98 million children that do not go to school every day in Africa as a mere statistical representation. The destiny of our children becomes a pile of files on a diplomatic desk somewhere. 'Foreign Aid' is something we get in exchange for good diplomatic ties with any nation that decides to pay temporary concern. We must learn to see Africa as the future, and especially, its leaders must learn to see the problems of our continent as the hungry, frail kid with no hope of livelihood. This out-of-date paradigm makes us see free and compulsory education only as a favour we offer to these children and not preferably as an investment into the future of our beautiful continent.

The single most important secret of development is to foster a society where everyone is free to express themselves in words and deeds in an environment that guarantees everyone's rights. The best place to begin such communities is in the classrooms. We could amaze ourselves with the results of such a world, for it is in the classrooms that superstitions and false thoughts can be replaced with inquiry and critical thinking.

Education is a fundamental human right for all and has been affirmed and continues to be reaffirmed by governments, non-governmental bodies, communities, activists, parents, and children. It was Kofi Annan who said that "Education is a human right with immense power to transform. On its foundation rests the cornerstones of freedom, democracy and sustainable human development."- But the fruit of this civil liberty continues to worm its way out of the hands of the children for whom this tree was planted and has begun to blossom.

Over two decades ago, the convention on the rights of the child received one of the highest known ratifications in human history, yet millions of children, particularly in the emerging world are denied these fundamental rights. Many more would live their lives without seeing a chalkboard or experience the joy of learning. Yet the vital decisions made in such countries are based on the assumption that such children who would later grow into adults are educated enough to interpret these policies and use them to implement development agendas. Nothing can be further from the truth!

Education for all children would continue to be seen as a burden to Africa and Asia's developing nations until all stakeholders redefine it. To begin walking in the light of this new knowledge is key to attaining all the seemingly unachievable sustainable development goals. The developing nations must realize that Education is the only road to El Dorado.

I would suggest you abandon any previous opinion you had about education. Let us assume you have stripped off your PhDs, title as Professor and every other name used to measure your intellectual accomplishments. One hundred and forty-one years ago, Thomas Edison's bulb first lit the streets of the United States, today you can talk to a loved one half across the world due to Alexander Graham Bell's invention which laid the foundation for modern telecommunication.

The ease with which antibiotics are prescribed makes us take the discovery of penicillin by Alexander Fleming and streptomycin (for tuberculosis, leprosy, and cholera) by Selman Waksman for granted. Every single comfort we enjoy, from the cup of instant coffee we wake up to, the electricity used to brew the coffee and keep our homes warm to all the contraptions of known and unknown inventors has given humanity the ability to experience life on a different platter. Now each of these advancements in human history was brought about by educated individuals. I must seize the chance to state that education does not necessarily connote passing through a classroom's four walls. Instead, it is a question of whether the lamp that leads the soul to truth has been lit or not.[3]

A shocking 258 million of our heroes and liberators are out of school in the world today. Many more do not even live long enough to see the light of day due to the heart-rending statistical accounts of infant mortality. Yet, these hold in their uncrafted minds; the solutions to humanity's problems. It is a paradox that they live their unproductive lives in societies that cannot support such loss of human resources. If only Africa, Asia and Latin America would realize that the solution to the challenges they face is not up in the skies, but in their children's minds, then maybe we would begin to see if only a glimpse of development.

What if Einstein was never introduced to the life-changing book by Aaron Bernstein on light and biology and its relationship to physics by a medical student who Einstein's parents hosted for dinner weekly or to the little geometry book which Einstein said transformed his understanding of the subject matter?[4]

Bernstein's books subsequently had a noticeable influence in helping Einstein formulate his theory of relativity as it gave him the necessary foundation and opened up his imagination. What if Alexander Fleming was not enlightened enough to notice a contaminating growth of fungi in his Petri dish which instead of throwing away, he investigated, leading to the development of antibiotics as we know it today? What if the Wright brothers had not been educated?

They would have remained at home making kites and fixing bicycles. If you take a close look at history and the contemporary social climate, you will discover a significant discrepancy between innovations in developed and educated societies with those in the emerging world.

Emerging world citizens who have enhanced quality of living were either immigrants or had to access education even if they had to fight their way through layers of discrimination and denial of opportunities. We cannot continue to blow trumpets for a few of our citizens who have broken themselves from this jinx. Such trumpets are not sonorous enough. We have to do all we can so that every child born in Africa is given a chance to liberate the continent and set it on its rightful place in the hall of honour of nations. The innovations extensively displayed by humanity's gallery of medals were wielded with blood, sweat and sacrifice of forebears into their children's lives.

It is widely known from deep down in African societies, that grassroots children are investments for the future. And it is on these words that we stand to peer over the wall of ignorance into tomorrow. By nature, humans hardly ever take seriously the wise words spoken to them by their parents, elders, and sages. We like to 'learn from experience.' Education is the only proven way humans can correct mistakes already made and prevent the fabrication of new ones.

The developing world must come together; and pool every resource available to free every child from mental and physical slavery. No nation should wait for this movement to be started synergistically. Every country must break the dam of reserved knowledge, expertise and potential in every child and youth. Africa's heroes and heroines die without a chance to try. No one can tap this resource for us. Human resources are not comparable to the oil in Nigeria and Libya or the solid minerals in the Congo. It is not like the Diamonds of southern Africa, and no one can claim to have the technical know-how to 'exploit' this unique resource. It can only be harnessed by the most willing hearts. This is a burden we must first carry ourselves, as we have seen. As developing nations depend solely on help from the international community, their children wallow in suffering. Their mothers cannot bear the look of hunger and despondency on the faces of their children. Children they bore to bring hope to them, and joy and peace to the world.

The effects of violating a child's educational rights are not felt instantly. The society in which that child finds himself only begins to feel the impact of the ignorant adult has become when he begins to exercise his right to survival through feeding, clothing, shelter, and raising a family. How such a disadvantaged individual meets these requirements are not always favourable to a nation's dream of attaining utopia. It is not uncommon to find a high rate of violence, prostitution, and crime syndicates; all of which are over-represented in the developing world.

When I was about eight years old, I remember being in primary school and there was a policy at the time by the ministry of education in Nigeria where state monitors or observers were sent mostly on unannounced visits to schools around Nigeria. I had this experience in Primary school, where I went to class and took notes in Mathematics. The pages of my notebook soon got to the very last leaf. And I checked the books in my bag, they were all filled up to the last line with my notes. I had forgotten to ask my parents for new notebooks. At that very instant of my dilemma, a woman walked in wearing spectacles that really defined her as an academician in my thoughts.

Without warning, the teacher shouted at the top of his voice for us to stand up. Like Policemen whose superior just walked into the parade ground unannounced, we got up to greet her with a jolt. It turned out it was the dreaded "Monitor" from the Ministry of Education. This one came all the way from the northern Nigerian state of Kano. She walked in and straight behind the class and sat down calmly.

I think she signalled the teacher to continue his lesson. We continued to take notes and solve equations. Finally, I wrote on the last page and immediately, my heart began to pump fast because she also started going round from seat to seat asking students' questions. So as not to seem idle, I turned to the cover of the book and continued my notes. I didn't know I was about to meet the first dedicated educationist in my life. As soon as she got to my seat, she looked at me, and cast one glance at the book and another at me. She screamed, "What is this?" "Teacher Felix, come here please!" and immediately, my nerves became frayed.

I was made to stand in front of the class, and then the bell for lunch break went off. The joy I felt was indescribable for one thing. I could take any embarrassment behind the eyes of my classmates but not in their presence. She went out, and my mind told me she was going to get a cane as this was the norm in Nigerian schools. The rod was indeed not spared in bringing us up as children in our clime, she asked the teacher to arrange a meeting with my parents the next day. When she returned, to my surprise, in her hands was a thick, new, fresh notebook. I couldn't hide my excitement and smile. When she handed it over to me, I said thank you and shook her hands.

When it was time to go home, I headed to the schoolyard entrance where parents usually wait to pick their children up. When I saw my Dad, he asked my siblings and me to wait a minute. He said his cousin was around and we were going to have lunch together. There is no need to say who this cousin was. It was a shocker for both of us- the "observer" from the Ministry of Education and me. To this day, I don't know if she had any discussion with my father about what had transpired in class that day, but I learned a great lesson.

Usman dan Fodio the Islamic promoter, writer, military strategist, and religious scholar as he is popularly known achieved many feats in West-Africa and shocked the world in many ways long ago in the 1800s. Today, his kinsmen and brothers, the Fulani nomads of Africa have not destroyed that legacy. They are great political lobbyists and politicians exuding a brilliance not found anywhere else on the continent. In my opinion, they have a record of academic excellence when given a chance. But what is their state and condition today? Do they run first-class laboratories and manage sky-bound corporations? Has the world given these ones a chance to try their ideas and concepts in solving health problems like HIV, Malaria and the sleeping sickness that predominantly trouble them? Or even the climate change that looms over our heads? Your guess is as good as mine.

Instead of mass education and progress, many of them still live in partially organized societies of cattle herders and nomads travelling on the back of the weather and chasing the rainy season and green pastures across west-Africa. Many of them have become easily influenced by get-rich-quick schemes, and in Nigeria, they are easy targets to be recruited into the terrorist group called Boko Haram. For those who escaped recruitment into terrorist groups, many have been involved in bloody struggles for fertile lands.

This has brought unprecedented carnage to the Nigerian society, and it is a classical agrarian battle as observed in other parts of the world at different points on the historical timescale. I firmly believe that this could be averted if most of them were provided free education in a way that suits their cultural norms, but it is a little bit more complicated than that. The solution to the challenges we face today is in the minds of the millions of Africans and Asians who die in their millions as the clock ticks in the world of curable ailments and artificial circumstances that challenge them in the world today.

The plight of even a single infant crying out of hunger or poverty is your problem. You may be living in Beverly Hills and probably own a few Haciendas all over southern America. But you are uncertain of what tomorrow may birth. We do not know the precise cause for all types of cancers now as I write this chapter today and we are not really close to total cures for many types of cancers, but we know there are many risk factors which is a tricky concept in epidemiology called causality nor do we have a final solution for the Covid-19 pandemic. We can salvage the answers to these questions and challenges by saving the human race's future, which is not something out there in some abstract compartment of our minds. It is right before our eyes, but as Goethe said, "the hardest thing to see is what is before our eyes." I believe that these children that we ignore are the ones with the potential to resolve these issues.

The goal of education is simple. However, to light up our minds; it is within our powers to let that light burn brighter, the extent to which the lights we hold would burn is, however, our sole responsibility. The goal of primary education in Africa would be attained the moment the aforementioned is actualized.

Our children should discover that books give them wings. If this is accomplished, there is no telling how far we can go. It would be a noble and a great thing for our children to have kaleidoscopic knowledge and perception of their world. The type that makes them inquisitive. There is nothing more important than this in the developmental journey of Africa.

The aim is to make African children brightly aware of their African environment and heritage. Only when we achieve this can we comfortably walk with our shoulders high in the global environment. This would open doors for Africans to indeed manipulate Africa's development climate for the better and greater good of all. Our real passage to true greatness. There is no access to the storehouse of continental wealth through the window. The door is widely open and welcoming but to access it, we must climb through hills. The cycle of thirst and satisfaction as far as learning is concerned is the crux of positive development. When it comes to education, it is better to view the world with a kaleidoscope than with a periscope.

As a child, I found it difficult to relate with girls even though they were always around me. Growing up, I had my way more with animals like our family's pet dogs, than I did with children of the opposite sex.

While growing up, I tried to dig deep into my mind's recesses to find out why this phenomenon made me really shy and a bit timid once I was around any gender that I could not associate with, play soccer with, wrestle with and try new bike stunts with. This is not to say that I did not have female friends who were my age grade and did all of the above even to the extreme that many boys will fear to tread into. I am not sure I have found the right answer to this question, but two things came to mind after years of introspection. The first one is that my two sisters did not come into my life during the early phase of my childhood and thus, I drew the conclusion that I was not socialized in a family setting with girls, therefore whenever I met them on the dirt roads and parks of Jos where we played, I did not have the right social decorum to relate with them. It was either I wrestled them too hard, or I got my back smacked on the floor terribly because I was too forgiving or simply because she was better than me. The second reason is that Nigeria is probably one of the top countries where the dichotomy between sexes is made very clear because of the social and cultural meme that has spread across the country spanning several generations.

In fact, we can say the same thing about most parts of Africa and the Middle East. Because I grew up in such a culture, I was not spared from this meme mostly. Anywhere you go in Africa except for countries like Rwanda which have made recent changes, you can see disparities in gender representation related to women and girls in schools, government parliaments, hospital staff, engineers and so on. However, when you make a count of the number of people touched by poverty and squalor, the women and children are the ones who fill up that room.

Humanity has reached a point where if we are to confront the environmental, health and technological challenges that confront us such as climate change and pollution, emerging infectious diseases and food security (the world population is set to reach 10 billion by 2050), we must look up to science as the force that will forge the way ahead for our species. As custodians of this planet and possibly our galaxy, we must look beyond the church's, synagogue's, and mosque's confines, to provide solutions to a world in chaos. A sound education is a tool that will sharpen the mind of future generations.

As I write this chapter in my cubicle in Switzerland, the whole world is battling with a coronavirus pandemic which broke out in Wuhan, China, in November 2019. The virus has brought the world to a standstill. Now everyone looks to the laboratories, doctors, epidemiologists, and microbiologists to find a solution for this carnage. The clergy are playing their part by providing spiritual comfort to millions who are troubled by this situation. But how are they doing it? Definitely not in their traditional buildings for fear of contracting this respiratory disease. They are employing information technology tools to do this through online services and calls to prayer. The great thinkers of these last centuries have warned us of the day when we lose our minds to religion and allocate the backseat to science and reason. No minds like I am sure is clear to you now are as fertile and impressionable. In difficult times and to solve problems, we must teach children right from the start to look inwards within their minds and apply deductive or inductive scientific tools to proffer solutions to the issues that may trouble them, the society, and the environment. The time has come for us to make the truth bare for all to see.

Many around the world argue that religion should be taught in schools. I think that this is complete nonsense. The problem with this type of thinking is that no one can decide which religion of the world should be taught in the classrooms. Science is a universal language that permeates the whole of nature from the smallest viral particle to the furthest reaches of outer space. The great astrophysicist Carl Sagan is often quoted as saying "Science is not perfect, it's often misused; it's only a tool, but it's the best tool we have. Self-correcting, ever-changing, applicable to everything: with this tool, we vanquish the impossible." I cannot state it in a more accessible way.

Carl Sagan during his life was a strong campaigner for the simplification and teaching of science in accessible ways to young people, particularly children and he created several TV series where he tried to instruct curious young minds on the kind secrets of science. This is not wishful thinking. I firmly believe that it is the only way to help us create a truly prosperous and sustainable life for everyone in the world. Religious education such as the Almajiri education and others which focus on teaching holy scriptures to the world cannot inform children of basic agricultural practices like crop rotation, equitable animal husbandry and basic economics to ensure their survival in a highly competitive world.

A world where resources are in abundance but remain artificially scarce because they have not been sustainably exploited. It is an eyesore to visit Brazil's favelas or the many ghettos in sub-Saharan Africa and not wonder why people scramble for morsels of bread when they could be trained to be service providers and at least gather enough knowledge to provide for their families.

The answer is simple, many of them missed the necessary knowledge transfer, which comes through a formal or informal science-based education. What do I mean by that? I am merely calling for applying the scientific method which involves; careful observation, the rigorous application of scepticism to analyse what is observed because a lot of bias can come from our minds when we try to make deductions from observations. It also involves the formulation of hypotheses through induction solidly founded on observation, then experiments may be carried out to test the hypothetical assumptions. The hypothesis generated is either accepted or rejected based on the experimental findings.

This method was developed in the 17th century based on empirical thinking. If these methods are taught to children worldwide, superstition and wishful thinking will slowly be shown the door out of our societies. The result would be a world where hunger is no more, the climate is stabilized, pollution is brought down to a level that the planet can conveniently and naturally deal with, and this will give peace a chance to reign through the four corners of the world.

The eyes of children radiate hope, love, and peace for us all. There is no way we shouldn't give them what they desire. Our lives and our actions should reflect consensus. Just like children make it seem, and like we once lived each day of our lives, the beauty of childhood never ends. No child chooses his path. In childhood, there is peace. To find this path that children show us, it is sometimes necessary to listen to their questions and reasoning. It is then that we see what we should reflect and who we should be. To them and to us. The peace that comes from within. It is more than hope, in fact. It is palpable that we can always be children . Or at least, we can choose to behave like them.

It is a good thing. Nothing short of miraculous that the paradise of childhood is never lost. We find it always. We only have to choose to relive the virtues that come naturally in childhood even as adults as many times as we have the opportunity to. Children of the universe are part of the universe too. While the world remains an open book, we are blinded by the different paradigms and the other garments in which the storytellers come. It remains true, however, that whoever listens, whoever searches would find it. Humans can be very loving people if given a chance to do so.

Don't children teach us this every day? Many may say it is a childish perspective to look at things this way. However, time has shown that it is this very perspective that wins. There is one reason to ensure that children are listened to. It is as stated above. Children speak many languages that we have either forgotten or that we refuse to speak. It is a beautiful language that has refused to be killed with descriptive words. There are simply not enough words to capture this magic language. It is a language that is beyond words. When they choose to make us understand, they use words. Every child should have the chance to view the world through a kaleidoscopic paradigm. A good education provides the opportunity. No child should be denied the chance to use this tool.

All a man's enemies are in his heart. Heaven is what you give to others. I remember being in class writing my final exams many years ago to the sound of gunshots while a religious war was being fought on the streets of Jos in Nigeria. Everything stank of war and of peril only. I did not feel like going on with education because staying alive was more important. I had no business with the war that was ongoing, but my mind was in two places. I was writing, and I was fighting at the same time in my mind. Children and youths worldwide want a favourable environment that permits them to lead the way towards development when their time comes.

I still vividly remember how our ancestry was traced step by step by our social studies teacher. Right from him explaining how humans evolved from the ape Australopithecus species, right down to Homo sapiens much to our chagrin. The teacher, each time looking at our faces to see how we were taking the news. And we, looking bewildered at one another. Swallowing these shocking revelations gradually. When we finally got to Homo sapiens, we were all relieved, but many of the etymological patterns in the evolutionary tree network made for new inside jokes. Many of us got new nicknames that day.

For the next few years, I would take it upon myself to school myself on man's origin on this planet. This quest lasted well into my university days and is still very interesting to me, and what I have been able to glean so far is astounding. I only have more respect for Charles Darwin. How could a single man have borne so much of a burden, overcoming our little enemies; procrastination for example and then tumbling on something as great and wonderful as the scientific theory of evolution and Natural selection? Many fields benefited from this unearthing. For example, studies of antibiotic resistance, production of insulin for diabetes management using bacteria instead of the gruesome process of extracting pig's insulin, understanding many diseases such as HIV, flu viruses, coronaviruses to mention a few. A fascinating observation is that almost everything in Darwin's life gradually prepared him and set the stage for this ground-breaking leap in science. From a short stint in medical school to his mastery of geology. From his senseless fascination with beetle collecting and taxonomy to his training to be a clergyman.

Everything was a carefully placed block to the finding that will revolutionize biology, medical sciences, and the way we think. These are the blocks we must establish for the world's children so that their path is as smooth as possible towards sustainable victory for our species.

Little wonder, the old man said: "Anyone who dares waste one hour of his time, has not discovered the value of life." One good culture that spreads across Africa's length and breadth is that a child is always a child of the community, and everyone plays a role in raising this individual to his full capacity. I think the rest of the world can learn from this shared communal responsibility in raising the future generation.

I believe that this culture originated from the value placed on children since many children died from various infectious diseases such as cholera or measles. So, everything had to be done to ensure their survival and integration into the larger society. It is an unorganized welfare system that cannot be monitored since it is impossible to track all minors and follow their social conditions till they become adults. Would it be possible then to have a hybrid form of this social system in which the government and the community are both involved in its minor citizens' welfare? Can social responsibility like childcare centres be set up and adequately managed using this system? It is evident that you care about children for you to have picked up this book. In my opinion, many folks care about children without having the courage to address these issues.

They forget that courage itself is fear with different attire. Sometimes, we don't have enough social skills to interact with them and consequently improve or innovate new policies for children in Africa, the Middle East or Asia. However, this is the only way to go ahead and make life bearable for children going through tumultuous times across the globe today.

We must all come together to debate and discuss these issues so that implementable policies can be developed around our immediate environment in the long run. However, the great question remains; thus, how can we establish social behaviours to protect children in the context of the 21st century without disrupting the kaleidoscopic nature and the fabric of the society, its pluralistic nature, and cultures. Like I have said previously, we could all become more sensitive to the happenings and plight of these children, to the existing child-focused policies and with some effort, we can all make a positive difference within our little individual spheres of life.

Several approaches can be taken to improve learning outcomes and school participation in regions of the world that have seemingly been left behind by the train of quality education. Yet I believe that the system can be efficiently transformed to catch up with the rest of the world. First, teachers are the backbone of students' learning, and when teachers do not fare appropriately as seen in many countries in Sub-Saharan Africa, a negative correlation is also found with pupil's overall performance. This may be linked to lack of motivation by the instructors who often spend the little they earn on some of their pupil's learning materials. The problem, therefore, is multifaceted.

I am only scratching the surface of the iceberg. In some studies[5] carried out in India, it was found that bonus payments to teachers based on the average performance or improvement in student learning performance were a significant factor that led to the success of many students.

This approach might kill two birds with a single stone.

The communities who implement such a system would no longer have to worry about the teachers' welfare or the performance of the students. Again, students' performance and teacher welfare are correlated, only this time positively. Secondly, the time spent in school learning needs to be improved. This does not necessarily mean increasing teaching time, but it mainly concerns areas where school attendance is low.

There are several methods which I have considered from reflection, research, and my experience from an impoverished society which I propose could work. I have discussed with many people who often say that improving the theoretical content and method of teaching might improve school attendance.

This is not always true because many children in communities of low and middle-income countries are willing to learn, but they often face barriers which could be environmental, logistic, or financial. I knew children who had to take care of cattle or other livestock and attend school at the same time or for some of them, they got to school without having breakfast because their families could not afford to feed them three times a day and the first meal was skipped, and only dinner was prioritized. These are all issues that could be tackled head-on if we solve these problems or at least attempt to. The teaching style and curriculum is a matter for another discussion.

First, we want to get the children to school, right? So, let's do that. First, the most obvious solution would be to set up school feeding programs, as I explained previously. The provision of conditional cash transfers to families who enrol their children in schools have also been tested,[5] and some countries have implemented it. However, it needs to be given more weight in the equation because it drives up the numbers of school attendance by making the problem a communal problem with shared responsibility between families and the government.

Now, to effectively confront the problem of pedagogy, we can start by making or at least ensuring that teaching rises to a kind of a professional status where only the most gifted and the most emotionally intelligent will be recruited to steward. It should be gratifying too to attract the most talented individuals. Teaching is intellectually stimulating and can have rewards for instructors again as has popularly been stated by

Richard Feynman, we teach so that we may truly learn. In Uganda, the headteacher in a primary school receives 814 000 shillings (about 215 dollars) per month even after a 30% increase by the government in 2019 while in countries in the global north where teachers are also more motivated to stay on the job and exert their most positive influence on students, the difference is glaringly shocking. In Sweden, a primary school teacher receives around 33 900 kronor (3325 dollars) per month. For some perspective, the average salary across all sectors in Sweden is about 34 600 Kronor. Would you like to guess which country has better students' performance among these two examples? No, don't waste your time.

This is what I mean by valuing the teaching profession and making it attractive for the most gifted in society. Great masters were often once disciples of other great masters. Alexander the Great was once a student of Aristotle, who was a student of Plato. Plato was a student of Socrates. You shouldn't be surprised by the influence each one had on Western thought flow, just like how water flows from the roots to the fruits in vineyards.

If the sacred task of instructing our future generations on how to thrive in an ever-changing environmental, economic, and socio-political world is left to the hands of semi-qualified and amateur intellectuals, we should not be surprised if the gains of enlightenment disappear from this sphere. Life is becoming increasingly competitive and complex. The tools we learned and use today to navigate the world and control the elements would not necessarily serve the next generation. This is because they will live in a different society. Therefore, we must ensure that children get instruction and tutoring from the very best in the community wherever they may be in the world.

We cannot leave this to chance or charlatans. How do low and middle-income countries or nations with faulty educational systems build the bedrock of their countries? This is no simple question to answer, and economists and political scientists have carried out studies and tested models to discover the most viable and productive method that can be employed to allow these impressionable minds to unfold in beautiful ways like a flower blossoming in spring. Here, one example that is worthy of mention is the Finnish system, which might help me convince you.

Forty years ago, in a bid to transform its economy, Finland reformed its educational system in a way that saw its ratings rise astronomically. The OECD has an initiative called the program for international student assessment (PISA). Among their peers from 32 countries, 15-year-old- Finnish students performed wonderfully in scientific literacy, mathematical literacy and reading literacy.[5] The students showed the best performance in reading literacy while in mathematical literacy, they were in the best quarter. After Japanese and Korean students, the students were found in the highest ranks again, scoring at the same level as students from the United Kingdom, Canada, New Zealand, and Australia. Today, adult literacy in Finland is arguably one of the highest globally, and they continue to be a formidable force in technological, social, and environmental advances.[6]

One other thing worth mentioning is that there is really no need to trouble young students' minds with meaningless tasks in real life. Time is a precious commodity. The ability to retain and utilize information dwindles with age. Everything we ask a child to do in class must be worth doing—no point assigning tasks to a child that would make the child feel like a permanent failure from the outset. Lessons should be customized to each child's abilities. When I was in primary school, I learned many things and was made to undergo mind-boggling tests that only served to concretize my fears in subjects such as mathematics.

In Finland for example, there are no mandated tests imposed on students until the end of their high school years unlike in most other parts of the world such as in the United States or in Japan or China. In essence, the national curriculum should not annihilate the imaginations of our children. Many of them in sub-Saharan Africa were made for the colonial era, and they are still in use. Such curricula were aimed to train Africans to be servants to their European masters without considering their own inborn creativity and intellectual freedom. The idea was for them to become clerks, secretaries and at best assistants to their masters. I know that many reforms have taken place since then in such countries' educational sector, but it is simply not enough. The kind of education children need to acquire should carry the spirit of their identity. This would enable them to stand tall and engage the international community rather than interacting with it from a borrowed perspective.

C H A P T E R

5

ERASING THE GENDER DICHOTOMY

———

"I've always believed that when you educate a girl, you empower a nation." -Queen Rania of Jordan

When I first heard that a girl fighting for the rights of the girl-child to acquire education in Afghanistan was shot and left for dead in October 2012, I was heartbroken like many around the world. Even when I found out that Malala Yousafzai had been flown to the United Kingdom for treatment after a gunshot at close range by the Taliban pierced through her skull while she was in a school bus, I could not muster any hope and I remained very pessimistic of her chances of survival for weeks. I was also disappointed, and my hope in humanity dwindled like a candle flame in a storm. Thankfully, she did survive the ordeal. The joy that surged through my spine and limbs when I saw the news on BBC that her surgery was successful is something I would always remember. As details from the story began to trickle in, I could not hide my admiration for the unmatched courage of this young girl. She was not even afraid when the Taliban terrorist had pointed his gun at her, and even the events that led to this final confrontation were dramatic.

Upon reflection and when asked what she thought of doing when a gun was pointed at her for her activism, she responded, It would be better to plead, "Okay, don't shoot me, but first listen to me. What you are doing is wrong. I'm not against you personally. I just want every girl to go to school." And this statement makes all the difference. As simple as it sounds, it is filled with a lot of yearning for girl-child justice and hope for the future of the world's children. Many girls have been disenfranchised and forced into early marriages, domestic labour, many have become victims of ancient traditions that have put them at the mercy of males and the society. In some countries of the world, it is a difficult thing to be born a female. That could spell the beginning of a sorrowful and challenging life.

Currently, around 132 million girls are out of school, in the world with sub-Saharan Africa making up almost 40 percent of these terrible statistics. Given that the region has been bedevilled with several socioeconomic challenges' ab initio, it makes economic and moral sense that African leaders make educating girls a priority while not ignoring boys. But the problem of illiteracy and semi-literacy disproportionately affects girls compared to boys in Africa, and this is valid for almost every other region in the world.

According to the Human Rights Watch, and as I have personally witnessed in Nigeria, or in other sub-Saharan African countries like Chad, Mali, Niger, Ghana, Senegal and Ivory Coast amongst others, 40 percent of girls are married off before their 18th birthday with these African countries accounting for most of the countries with the highest levels of the sore global child marriage share.

Sadly, the region makes up a large part of the world's prevalence of adolescent pregnancies with as high as 51 percent of girls giving birth before turning 18 thus jeopardising their health, education and socioeconomic welfare in their communities. Some of the factors that influence this trend include religion and culture which more often than not stigmatise pregnant or unmarried girls, leading to a sharp, sustained spike in the number of young girls forced into early marriages. Thus, it is no surprise to anyone watching this phenomenon that thirty-three percent of girls from the world's poorest households have never seen the walls of a classroom.

There is no way to overstate the importance of educating girls. There are a myriad of positive reasons to focus on improving girl child education and ensuring that this gender is not spared the adverse effects of illiteracy such as poverty, poorer health outcomes, uninformed life choices which could jeopardise their position in the society they live in and at the global stage. Millions of adult women in the world today have been silenced, their voices and dreams buried with them when they die, because they were not lucky enough to get through the four walls of a classroom or even capable of reading or writing. Since boys were often the favoured gender in the Idoma ethnic group which I belong to in Nigeria as is true in many African families, and because these families believed that boys were more capable of bringing economic returns to their homes and communities compared to girls, my maternal grandmother was denied access to education. At the same time, her brothers were allowed to attend school.

She often told us that she wished she was educated and knew how to speak the several languages taught at school, such as English. She spent one long period of her adulthood attending classes in the evenings to make up for lost times which made me consider her a courageous woman.

Knowing the importance of education, she ensured that all her girls and boys, including my mother, my uncles and aunties, completed their education. She prioritised education and made many sacrifices, ensuring that her children never went to school hungry or that their needs were left unmet. In my case, when I told her that I planned to do a doctorate degree in epidemiology, she prayed for me regularly and continued to encourage me to give it my best efforts until she sadly passed away in 2020 after health complications associated with ageing.

She is my hero, and she was confident that education can improve any person who tastes the Pierian spring, and such a person could bring positive social change in the society which the world is in dire need.

Society can benefit in enormous ways from educating girls and women, especially in developing economies where this problem seems to be most prevalent. Education has always been a tool for the empowerment of individuals, and it is no different in the case of girls who are plagued by various forms of inequality and lack of access to education or information that could positively transform their lives and free them from future poverty and deprivation.

Educating girls in developing regions of the world, such as in Africa, ensures that they can make informed choices on the lives they wish to lead as their future unfolds. Considering the structural and societal injustice girls and women have suffered, they deserve healthier and happier lives, this is enough reason to justify their education. However, it seems that these fundamental reasons include the fact that the Convention on the Rights of the Child tries to convince us of these directions for girls' lives, these reasons do not sink through the depths of many people's hearts in the world today. What do we do then since this is an urgent matter? It is not just a matter of social justice, but it also makes economic sense for many developing countries in Africa, such as in the north-west region of Nigeria, where this problem has taken root. Educated girls and women possess information, life skills and the confidence to positively impact their communities by being better parents, technocrats, and citizens. For example, the fertility rate of women in north-eastern and north-western Nigeria where many women are uneducated averages eight children per woman while in the south of Nigeria where women are more likely to attend school, it peaks at four children per woman.

As[8] being shown by various social scientists in different settings and in different countries, this means that educated girls can choose to marry later in life and have few children. An educated girl is also more likely to bear children who will survive the dangerous childhood infections, starvation, and drowning. Education also improves the productivity of women at their jobs and enables them to earn better. The return on education is more interesting, economically speaking for girls than for boys to a slight extent.

Several studies from some countries show that a year of schooling has the power to increase a woman's future earnings by around 15 percent compared to 11 percent for a man[9]. This is absolutely fantastic because it is in line with the age-old African proverb; "If you educate a man, you educate an individual. But if you educate a woman, you educate a nation." However, it is surprising that this wisdom is not applied in many African nations, especially in sub-Saharan Africa and in some southern African countries. I think it is time we all look into the mirror and listen to our ancestors' gentle pristine voices, trying to guide the continent to redemption and what seems like an economic el Dorado.

However, the importance of girls' education to public health and their individual health is well recognised by health scientists and sociologists. This truth seems to evade the sight and conscience of the vast majority of the world today, especially in impoverished regions in sub-Saharan Africa. However, I would like to reiterate clearly in this book that there is a strong association between education and health outcomes of girls, women, babies, and families.

The more educated one is, the more likely they would prioritise the healthcare of their families and seek the right kind of medical attention for the myriad possible diseases that could bedevil them. Educated women are also better informed in preventing diseases such as diarrhoeal diseases, and some genetic diseases like sickle cell anaemia by avoiding sexual relationships with a sickle-cell allele carrier. Also, girls who are educated in their earlier years are usually able to earn more as I have already mentioned previously, but this also means that they will be able to afford health services and know-how to obtain at least basic health insurance.

I once witnessed the pains of a girl called Amina who was suffering from sickle cell anaemia in my birth town of Vom, Nigeria. She was only a few days shy of her 7th birthday when I heard that she was sick. I did not know that she had this genetic disease which is an adaptation of the human body to the malaria parasite in which the red blood cells become sickle to avoid being infected with the parasite. The downside of this evolutionary adaptation is that the red blood cells cannot sequester enough oxygen, causing an asphyxiating experience for the sufferer. On that day, she was having a sickle cell crisis and found it very hard to breathe. Her limbs and nervous system were also shutting down fast. She could not get herself to stand or walk.

Not appreciating the gravity of the situation, her family called on their church pastor's services to save her. This was probably because it was cheaper than going to the hospital or they were poorly informed about what to do, which would not have been the case if they were highly educated and informed. Unfortunately, this was not the case for this family. Sadly, for Amina, after the pastor had prayed all evening and she still failed to walk, he told her mum that the girl was deliberately refusing to walk, and he quickly left the scene as the situation became worse.

The family believed his words and tried to cajole the little Amina to walk and get over her crisis. Even though her mum was ready to do anything for her beloved daughter that evening, she did not think it was necessary, nor did she have the money to take her to the hospital.

Her mother dropped out of secondary school when she became pregnant with Amina's older sister. Many people in Africa rely on the services of charlatans and seers to solve their health problems, and the driving force for this is the resource and information constraints that they face in the family which a good knowledge of education would have been valuable. Many of these families cannot afford essential health care services, even if it costs a few dollars. This is peculiar to Africa or impoverished regions of the world. In the United States, (one of the most developed economies in the world), communities such as the black communities record low educational enrolments. Many studies have suggested that families from these communities have higher rates of teenage pregnancy and inability to afford health services particularly health insurance. However, the topic of health services financing in the United States is more complicated than I have painted here.

Girls' sexual and reproductive health is one aspect of health that is significantly impacted by education in an almost direct relationship. For example, human papillomavirus (HPV) is the most common sexually transmitted infection passed through the skin-to-skin contact and can affect the genitals, mouth, or throat of infected individuals. Although not all infection cases with HPV lead to medical complications, some do lead to cancers of the cervix, anus, or throat. Thankfully, it is effectively prevented through vaccination.

Still, an estimated 100 000 women are diagnosed with cervical cancer in sub-Saharan Africa even though it is preventable. One of the explanatory variables in this equation is the low uptake of sexual health education in this geographical region. In a recent study in China, students were randomly assigned to two different groups, an intervention group and a control group with the intervention group receiving a power-point health education seminar as well as completing questionnaires after the symposium.[10]

A year later, after both groups completed the same questionnaire, although the level of knowledge retained from the study declined a few percentages, students in the intervention group were still more willing to be vaccinated against HPV and were more aware of the necessary information about the cause of cervical cancer. This means, given regional and cultural differences between China and Africa, if sexual health education is correctly integrated into the curricula of schools, girls and boys can learn the material in the schools in the case that they manage to attend school; we could really make significant progress in curbing several sexually transmitted infections that cause people to go through untold suffering and stigma.

A predominant health complication due to pregnancy is often seen in many parts of Northern Nigeria is called Vesico Vaginal fistula or simply known as VVF in which young girls usually between the ages of 11 to 15 get pregnant with their pelvic region not being not being large enough for them to have a natural birth at that age. And in the case where they are attended to by unskilled birth attendants who simply rush the moment and are clueless about what medical procedure to undertake, these unskilled local midwives simply cut through the vagina to bring out the child.

This result is constant unregulated leakage of faeces and urine by these girls or women, which leads to these girls becoming outcasts in their communities. For instance, Nigeria has the highest prevalence of Vesico Vaginal Fistula (VVF) globally, with around 800 000 women living with this condition with as high as 90 percent of the cases left unattended. Most of these cases are in the northern region of the country where child marriages and low-level education are ubiquitous. These uneducated girls, have no professional information on how to manage their pregnancy.

They are usually influenced by their religious leaders who usually expressly warn them not to go to a healthcare centre to give birth to their children, but to do so in a church or in an Islamic setting because they consider children to be gifts from God. A Nigerian academic once reported the case of an 11-year-old Nigerian girl who became pregnant but received no antenatal care due to her church's influence who insisted that the baby should be born in the church.[11] She received no antenatal care until her date of delivery arrived. While suffering a two-week long labour, she was tossed back and forth between unskilled traditional birth attendants, faith healers and the church.

Someone eventually forced a stick through her mouth to the abdomen where the baby was ultimately forced out revealing a decomposing dead body. She had to suffer twenty repair operations in four years to correct the damage her body suffered, and she never recovered fully back to her previous healthy state before all the charade began. This story is not unique; sadly, many girls and their families, rendered powerless by a lack of access to education, fall victim to religion when it comes to making their health choices. Education is a formidable tool to erase gender-related problems and discrimination, which disproportionately affects girls, and that is strengthened along the lines of gender dichotomy.

It is now a known fact that gender inequality is highly prevalent in developing economies. However, emerging economies by no means wield a monopoly on gender equality. Women earn less than men in almost all countries and in most sectors of the economy from agriculture to sports and acting.

These, however, may be more ingrained in some cultures of the world rather than others. The appearance of suppression of females often precedes gender-based discrimination, violence, and inequality. In 2015, economist Seema Jayachandran showed that Gross domestic product (GDP) per capita correlates with inequality in education, health, and tolerance of gender-based violence.

The lower the GDP per capita, the more likely these forms of social injustice were perpetrated. Is economic underdevelopment responsible for the various forms of discrimination women face worldwide?[12] Is there a causal association between economic underdevelopment and these indices of gender-based discrimination, or are there other factors involved? When nations start their developmental journey, the economic sector is usually based on brawn (strength)-based production for which men have an anatomical and physiological advantage.

This does not remain the case as countries progress towards an economy based on services delivery where women have more mental capacity and are at an advantage. According to Javachandran, "if men specialise in brawn-based occupations and women in brain-based occupations, then at early stages of development boys will receive more education than girls. As brain-based sectors grow, girls should catch up." As far as I know, many emerging economies are still stuck in brawn-based production systems where boys and men are overwhelmingly favoured over girls and women in the economy and social strata. But this is not all there is to this story.

Along with religious beliefs or practices, some cultural factors are also to blame for these disparities in gender equality and prolong erasing the gender dichotomy. For example, most African spirituality is designed to oppress women from the cradle to beyond the grave. An African man asserts his power over women by marrying as many wives as possible while exerting control over their bodies and will. This is supported by the communities in which these women dwell.

Many of these women cannot look beyond the confines of this paradigm of oppression since it is the only culture they know and were born into. For example, ancestral spirits from a father's side of an African family are given more importance than ancestral spirits from the mother's side of a family, and many female spirits in African cultures are associated with evildoing rather than strength and progress. The only way women are empowered in such societies is when a woman is possessed by a spirit and becomes a medium. This gives her power and status in the community and attests that there is still hope for redeeming the millions of girls and women trapped by societal dogma into pervasive servitude. I do not mean that we have to somehow figure a way to make all girls possessed.

What I refer to, is that deep within the hearts of many Africans there is a place for the girl child or women in the society that is revered, but that has been relegated to the background of the scheme of things in these communities. The fact that a possessed woman wields power and is respected means that we can also convince them otherwise that girls are just like boys even if they don't like to jump from heights into shallow streams or always play in the dirt.

Religion has played a crucial role in many African countries' organisations since the arrival of European Christians and the Islamic conquerors of North Africa and many parts of West Africa. Both Christianity and Islam can be justly apportioned blame in the existential perception of many Africans today, primarily on how they handle girls and women. In the creation account of the bible and in a letter by Paul the convert apostle to the Corinthians, it is clearly implied that a man is the head of a woman, since man preceded woman in the earth's creation account in the bible. Islam[13] has not fared any different to African women and girls. The climax of the role religion plays in suppressing women can be seen in today's Nigeria where the terrorist group "Boko Haram" (meaning 'Western education is a sin') has used terrorism to instil fear in the hearts of many families from the far north to the deep coastal regions of Nigeria in the south.

They have been involved in kidnapping of school students like the 200 girls kidnapped in Chibok, Nigeria, which sparked international protests and campaigns under the hashtag #BringBackOurGirls and this was supported by the then First Lady of the United State of America Michelle Obama. Since then, their attacks on schools have become more familiar with a particular loathing for girls attending schools. In their philosophy, girls should be married off at an early age and made to bear children.

The surprising thing about this sad phenomenon is that some Muslims in the northern part of Nigeria sympathise with the idea of suppressing girls and the general apathy towards formal education with parents often preferring to send their children to Islamic schools to become Almarijiri's roaming the country as I have earlier mentioned in a previous chapter. Even when girls are not expressly oppressed, many girls born to Islamic families in Nigeria are often denied access to education since their destiny is tied to an early marriage as stipulated by the family's religious beliefs. There is thus no motivation to educate them since they will soon belong to another man's family, and therefore there is no express need in the mind of their parents for an investment in their education. It is like cancer that makes a comeback after every remission in retrogression in progress made in combating gender inequality on the continent.

It would well be within the bounds of reason to argue that education is the fundamental right of all girls in the world and indeed all boys no matter what country they might be citizens of or where they live with their families. The United Nations Convention on the Rights of the Child, which came into force in 1990, explicitly spells out every human child's rights. The Convention on the Rights of the Child affirms that every child has a right to education.

And that the purpose of education is to enable the child to develop to his or her fullest possible potential and to learn respect for human rights and fundamental freedom.[14] As of 2020, 196 countries have ratified this convention, including every member of the United Nations except the United States of America. Many African countries, including developing economies of the world in Sub-Saharan Africa, are parties to this convention at least on paper. In reality, however, it seems to be a severe challenge for many of these countries to implement from the top down to the grassroots to impact every child's life.

This disparity is most often seen in how many girls are denied access to education across these countries and communities. Although not perfect yet, it is generally the status quo that boys go to school while girls are involved in other tasks required by their families until they are married off most times forcefully to bear children and continue their lives otherwise. Can we then say that this Convention on the Rights of the Child is full of idealistic hope and nothing more? Even when girls in Africa have access to education, they are usually guided by their families, teachers, every adult who can influence them and society into specific fields such as the arts and humanities and they are often discouraged from taking courses in Sciences, Technology, Engineering and Medicine (STEM). As a result, there is an under-representation of girls in various fields of science and science education, especially girls of African descent.

As an epidemiologist, I have attended several global health conferences where the panels discussing girls' health, especially sexual and reproductive health, were chaired by males. In fact, most times, the entire panels would consist of males only, however, occasionally the inclusion of one woman who most likely is bullied into silence by men who speak with the authority of having the numbers seems to soothe the conscience of the organisers. From the perspective where girls in developing countries need role models who can model their lives after or mentor them, they are left with nothing and thus see the sciences as a field that only men are good at. Girls need to have female role models in STEM who can inspire their hearts and challenge their intellect, spurring them into action and dedication in their academic pursuits to take upon leadership roles in the communities and on the global stage.

The inequality in STEM has a long history and has occurred in almost every country and region of the world since the Middle Ages when the pursuit of knowledge got an infusion of a second wind. There are many aspects to it from the family's level to policies made in national governments' executive offices. We are all responsible for this menace. It starts with the toys we buy for children according to what we hold in our minds as appropriate for their genders. Girls are usually gifted dolls while boys are given toy stethoscopes and trailers. The failure and inability of governments of emerging economies to implement the resolutions reached at the Convention of the Rights of the Child's mandate when it comes to the girl child is disturbing and condemnable. As mentioned above, health sciences is just one aspect that is out of balance.

There aren't enough girls in the health sciences even after centuries of formal education. Even in developed economies where the underrepresentation of girls in STEM is less conspicuous, many of these countries have had to deal with centuries of female suppression in knowledge acquisition and are still in the process of correcting these deficits. It means that if Africa is to take its place in the global arena, it must begin the process to overtake the West.

For example, in France and in many developed countries, it was formerly imagined that girls could not perform well in the medical sciences. However, recent statistics from the French Ministry of Higher Education, Research and Innovation revealed that girls perform equally good as boys if not better and often excel more than boys in medical school exams. According to the French Ministry, 64 percent of students in medical, dental, and pharmaceutical programmes between 2015 and 2016 were women, a 3.1 percent rise from 10 years ago.

But it wasn't always progress and glory for the French. The French government has actively introduced laws which it continues to review supporting girls and women who wish to continue work or school after childbirth. It takes the belief and acting on the mantra that education is a fundamental tool for development and the key to erasing the gender dichotomy in the world for such level of development to occur in any country of the world for girls and women.

Wherever we may find ourselves, we should all put our voices together to build momentum for this movement of advocating for girls' rights. Although developed countries started the noble race to educate more girls with a clear advantage over emerging economies, thankfully, the gap is closing between these two economic regions of the world-the global north and south. As of 1970, girls were already attaining an average of 11.5 years of education in high-income countries, and as of 2019, it has gone a little bit above 17 years while low income developing countries who started at almost zero years of education have been able to secure 8.9 years of education for girls with these girls gradually spending more time in school.[15] In sub-Saharan Africa and in Northern Africa, girls' mean school duration has more than doubled from 3.3 years to 8.8 years and 5.3 years to 12.7 years respectively since the 1970s.

Even though these statistics bring some form of hope for development workers and human right's activists, sub-Saharan Africa is still far behind its set goal of providing 12 years of universal primary and secondary education to girls as part of its Sustainable Development Goal number 4. This target is a commitment to providing 12 years of quality education to girls and boys by 2030. According to data from the UNESCO Institute for Statistics, 50 years ago, a girl born in Burkina Faso would have received just one year of education whereas this has risen to 8.7 years of education today.

In Nigeria, South Sudan, Chad, Mali, Niger and the Central African Republic, girls still struggle to see the four walls of a classroom, while one third of girls of primary school age are out of school. We must not allow this sad story to linger on in our world because we have the power to do something positive about it by starting little no matter where we may be and on whatever level of the economic ladder we might be on. Many girls know that education is the portal to redemption and fulfilment of their dearest dreams. It could give them the necessary information to fight archaic cultures of female suppression like female genital mutilation, gender-based violence and the general pervasive culture of oppression against women prevalent in many emerging countries. But these girls also know that they cannot wait for adults to get their act together and wave a cosmic magic wand that will make all their problems disappear in a whiff. That is why several of them have taken to campaigning for their rights to education, better livelihoods for girls and women, and security of their bodies and minds in a male-dominated world.

Malala Yousafzai was only ten years old when the Taliban came to her village in Pakistan. Within months of their arrival and according to the laws of Shariah which they propagated, they claimed that watching TV and listening to music or dancing were responsible for earthquakes and were banned by them on the threat of severe punishment.[16] These men were Kalashnikov or sword-bearing men who stopped at nothing to administer violence to anyone who broke these rules. In compliance, most of the villagers destroyed their TV sets, DVDs, and CDs. But they did not stop at that, they also thought that girls should not attend school or get a formal education but should instead be in purdah (restricted to seeing only the closest members of their families and draped in coverings) because this was contrary to the teachings of the Holy Quran. But Malala would not give up on going to school and encouraged other girls to remain in school despite all the restrictions that were imposed by the Taliban. As the months went by, she became quite well known in her village to flaunt the rules and advocate for girl child education even if she was just a young girl.

Thus, she became a target for the Taliban who felt that if they could silence her through death, it would send ripples of fear through other girls' hearts in the region and accomplish their goals of preventing girls from attending school. One morning on October 9, 2012, Malala, 15 years old at the time, was finally shot by the Taliban. Unsuspecting of anything that morning, she was seated on a bus heading back home from the day's lessons at school and talking with her friends about schoolwork. Two Taliban men in a van stopped the bus, and a young, bearded Taliban asked: ***"Who is Malala?"*** She identified herself, worrying that harm should not come to her friends. The man fired three shots at her with one of the bullets penetrating her skull and lodged in her shoulder, putting her life in danger. She was airlifted to a military hospital in Peshawar, Pakistan and was transferred four days later to a specialist hospital in Birmingham, United Kingdom. Everything she suffered was simply because she and her family were determined that she gets an education even as a girl in a society that strongly resisted that form of progressive thinking. She was able to continue attending school in the UK after having undergone several successful surgeries.

She was later awarded the prestigious Sakharov Prize for Freedom of Thought and subsequently awarded the Nobel Prize for Peace with Indian children's rights activist Kailash Satyarthi. Malala has continued to advocate for girls' rights across the world, especially in developing countries speaking up for the unheard in these unseen regions of the world. She has travelled to Kenya and Northern Nigeria where she spoke against the abduction of the 200 Chibok girls by Boko Haram which is reminiscent of the Taliban with whom she had to contend in Pakistan. These two groups seem to share the same ideology aimed at preventing girls from attending formal education.

Malala is not a lone crusader in the fight for justice in girls' and women's lives. In almost all regions of the world, if you put your ears down, you can hear the drums of freedom being beaten by young girls doing everything in their power to make sure that their voices and outcries on the need for far-reaching social justice that many impoverished regions of the world lack. For example, in West Africa and sub-Saharan Africa, there is a growing, dynamic culture of social organising and activism by and for girls and young women.

Most of these young girl activists are involved in advocacy in the community, they organise seminars on gender-based violence, female genital mutilation, child marriage, education, orphans and vulnerable children and menstrual health, among others. Education plays a significant role in providing the platform for many of these girls to speak up because even when their voices are not stifled by a lack of education, many adults do not take them seriously. However, these adults are the very ones who need to listen to their sermons.

Jakomba Jabbie is a teenager from The Gambia who advocates for girls' access to education in her country, especially encouraging all actors to create opportunities for girls to be engaged in STEM. She started a robotics club in her school to encourage girls to try out science and technology. Latifatou Campaore is another teenager whose area of activism is against female genital mutilation. Empowered by her mother who was cut as a young girl in Burkina Faso, Latifatou's dream is to see that no girl's genitals are mutilated under any circumstances, and their sexual health freedom is not threatened.

If these kids can speak up even though their lives or place on the social ladder is threatened, you can also do so. Another blossoming female teenage voice is Zuriel Oduwole, a Nigerian American filmmaker who is also passionate about girl child education in Africa. She has been listed by Forbes magazine as one of Africa's most influential women. Having travelled to Ghana from the United States where she was born to shoot a documentary for a school project on the Ghanaian revolution, she met the late President Jerry Rawlings who led the revolution. She teaches girls how to tell their stories using the screen as her medium. She has spoken to many presidents and prime ministers about girl child education in Kenya, Namibia, Ivory Coast, and many others.

Educating a girl not only improves her life but also the lives of her family, community, and the society at large. Denying girls their right to education keeps many societies in the dark and at a disadvantage.[17]

Religion and culture are not permanent edifices in society that cannot be unmoved. They are subject to the winds of change for a reason. In African communities and indeed across the world, everyone can all work together to expunge the harmful effects of these societal constructs that continues to relegate girls to the back of the room and the lower castes of society. One way the ancient sages in African lands did this was through verbal telling of tales and fables that endured from century to century and still have vestiges in several modern African countries even till this present day.

As a young boy, besides the legends that my grandmother told my siblings and I, intending to plant subtle character-forming seeds of knowledge that could spring into moral guideposts in our lives as adults, it was also the usual thing at the time for children. Besides, the cartoons we looked forward to watching on television were also part of it. We were captivated by TV programs that consisted simply of an old man or woman narrating allegories and tales to children which was then telecasted across the country.

I now believe that besides the ability of those stories to make us travel through time and have wild imagination, one of the reasons why it sustained our curiosity and captivated our limited attention is the fact that we knew deep within that these stories would serve us well in the future.

Today, sociologists complain of the lost art of passing knowledge and wisdom through storytelling in Africa. Whether they were African, Asian, European, or North American children. We learned that all children were connected.

It didn't matter that some were boys or that some were girls. I credit experiencing my most fundamental knowledge of gender equality not through express statement to me, but rather, it was something I could infer from these stories. Today, this art is lost for most children in Africa as their lives are consumed by faster media, internet, TV, and other forms of accessing information which does not necessarily connect to the hearts of these children and pass knowledge about the beauty of gender equality and the roles that they can play as future adults in ensuring this positive value. Many parents in Africa instead wish for their children to acquire a religiously potent foundation in life, hoping that it will guarantee their success in life. But what does religion teach about gender equality? In Christianity, the very conception of the doctrine of the trinity and the fall of man through the actions of a woman would teach any child even subtly that women do not deserve any better in life since they are the cause of the fall of man from glory to the depths of suffering and calamity on earth. In Islam, women are not allowed in gatherings where men are found, and men are encouraged to "lightly" beat stubborn wives.

Whatever "lightly" means is left to your interpretation, but we all know too well that the promotion of any form of violence against women at any time in history and especially now in the 21st century is an absolutely unacceptable injunction. However, these and many worse things are what children learn passively in a religious setting coated with seemingly good morals that they can learn anywhere. Isn't it time for us to reform these traditions of violence and oppression against women and girls?

In Africa's past history and even today in some remote areas of the continent which managed to remain unscathed by too much influence from the colonial era, it is not uncommon to find women in leadership roles in the cultural fabric of their communities in which some of them hold chieftaincy roles under the mandate of their community's unique way of bestowing the title on them. Many of them lead with impeccable honour, and passion worth emulating by young girls and boys. Theresa Kachindamoto assumed office in 2003 as a paramount chief in the Dedza district of central Malawi wielding influence over close to a million people.

Born into a family of twelve children to a traditional leader in the region, and having five boys of her own, she was selected as inkosi or paramount ruler in the district because of her charisma and good relationship with people but also because she was the most senior leader at the time the selection was made. She was particularly disturbed when she found out that there were high rates of child marriages in her community amidst a worrying HIV epidemic.

Even though she has only male children, she was able to empathise with young girls who were forced into early marriages by the region's customs. Having worked in a college for more than a quarter of a century, she knew the benefits of education and how child marriages threatened the success and stability of the children involved. First, it was difficult to persuade the parents of the children involved because both the constitution and the traditional council's customary law stipulates that children could marry if their parents were in agreement.[18] Although it was difficult to persuade parents to disavow child marriage, she was able to convince 50 sub-chiefs in the Dedza district to agree to abolish child marriage. She set out to challenge these customs armed with nothing but her authority and knowledge about these situations and began firing sub-chiefs who were in support of child marriages while successfully annulling close to a thousand child marriages stating that education was more critical for those children.[18] She has since gained world fame as a defender of child rights and freedom of the human spirit. I consider her a fearless woman to have taken such a stance in African society, and her tenacity and will-power to go against the grain in favour of the well-being of the Malawian children under her care.

Her actions have inspired many non-governmental organisations and the international community. When you think about it, it is a beautiful thing to imagine what one person can do and how she has saved many present and future lives by her simple resolve. She is a modern-day example of how female African chiefs protect the rights of not just the girl-child but also the rights of everyone against the forces of patriarchal exclusion in all her glory. She will always be remembered as a bastion of hope for Malawi's children and for every living and unborn African child.

Africa's male and female children can be united and directed towards a life of victory and inspiration through the lost art of collective storytelling that shows the strengths of both genders and helps build a unifying history of them together. As I insinuated above, this singular and simple practice could enable them to see each other as equals rather than one sex hoping to dominate the other through archaic cultural traditions or religious fantasies.

In this digital age, it might be impossible to gather children under an Iroko tree on a moonlit evening to narrate tales to them. But as much as the era of the moonlit evening might have disappeared for most African children, the digital age comes with many ways in which creators and social entrepreneurs can change the narrative for these children and help to erase the gender dichotomy by bringing these stories to Africa's children in forms they can access. This could be through good scripting of cartoons, animations and other media meant to address these issues and delivered in a dynamic and paradigm-shifting manner. We could also implement this change through the kind of toys that are sold in the African market. We do not have to wait until girls have been married off or denied education or abused before we swing into action. The time to act is now-proactively since we are all well aware of the problem. And if you would take one key message from this book, it should be that; we can all act today on behalf of these children and not tomorrow nor the day after.

One fundamental action step that can be taken to eliminate gender inequality is to provide role models for girls and women who can raise the hopes and aspirations of the next generation of children. Marie-Curie, the two-time Nobel Laureate went to school when it was almost considered an abomination for girls to go to school. She ended up proving society wrong by winning two Nobel Prizes in Chemistry and in Physics.

It goes without saying that she is one of the most brilliant minds to have graced the surface of the earth. Today, millions of women are doing extraordinary things across the planet but who might have been forced to hide their lights under a bushel. They need to stand up proudly and become visible so that girls can light their candles from their flames of knowledge and success. Women also need to be encouraged to get more involved in local, regional, and international politics and hold positions of power. Truth be told, every day I watch the news, I see women doing well, making a political statement through their lives that they can even serve better in positions of power. Think of Ngozi Okonjo-Iweala who has chaired several national and international organisations such as the world bank, she is a former finance minister in Nigeria, she is presently the Director General of The World Trade Organization (WTO).

She is also served as the chair of the board of directors of the GAVI, the vaccine alliance, headquartered in Geneva, Switzerland, which is a fund set up to bring childhood vaccines to every child in the world. Or you could think of Jacinda Ardern, New Zealand's Prime minister who has guided her country successfully economically and through the Coronavirus pandemic with such finesse, humility. and knowledge. Girls need these figureheads.

One final step that could be taken is for girls and women's voices to be given a platform so they could express themselves independently in national and global decision making, which is somehow related to the previous point.

I have written a lot about girls in this chapter, and I believe that although it is justified to spend a lot of time talking about the travails of the girl child, if we ignore boys, we could have another problem brewing in the future in which boys themselves as men could become the very problems we are trying to prevent and conquer if we do not win them over now and fight for their rights as well. The gears of war, conflict, and chaos are greased by the blood and sweat of over 300 000 children who serve in organised government armies as child soldiers but mostly in rebel factions in unorganised warring guerrillas. Most times, they are boys. These children are spread all over about 20 countries today performing subservient tasks in armed conflict as active combatants, porters, cooks, sex slaves or in any task that they are conscripted into to push forward the political and economic goals of their lords of war. Although most of them are recruited in Africa, about 50% of recruitments take place far away in countries like Syria, Iraq, Colombia, and Myanmar.[19]

A walk through the rubbles of Aleppo or through the rain forest in the DRC (Democratic Republic of Congo) will fetch you many tears welling stories from children whose lives have been completely destroyed by their precious participation in armed conflicts. Children below the age of 18 are usually recruited into armed groups forcefully or by influencing them through the use of drugs and money. Their minds are fragmented into a thousand pieces that may never be put together just like a jar of Chinese porcelain which falls from a cliff unto rocks remains is altered forever. Many become lifelong illicit drug users and often consume cocaine, heroin, marijuana. and glue. As if that is not enough, their lives are at critical risk of infections such as hepatitis B and C, HIV/AIDS, gonorrhoea, and syphilis. The harm that armed conflict has on children transcends their lives into the lives of several generations after them. Images of ex-child soldiers are usually saturated with concepts such as post-traumatic stress disorder (PTSD), anxiety, depression. and suicidal tendencies. These themes seem to be one of the most recurring scenarios for most ex-child soldiers undergoing rehabilitation.

Many efforts are directed at refocusing their energies and interests to peaceful and productive concepts to participate in society like the children they are. Most of these programs are successful. It is really wonderful that several worldwide efforts continue to bring this evil practice to an end; like the prosecution of individuals and groups who foster it and deliver justice for these kids. In July 2019, the U.N. Security Council passed a resolution to "strengthen mechanisms to prevent violations against children." About it, the U.N. Special Representative for Children and Armed Conflict, Virginia Gamba said, "Today's resolution is providing us with important tools to better respond to the needs of boys and girls, such as the reintegration of former child soldiers," According to Child Soldiers International, about 55 000 children have been freed since 2013. However, over half of them are yet to receive reintegration support.

Some years ago, after watching the movie "Beasts of no nation", a conversation started between a friend and myself in which I first learned of Mohammed Sidibay, a child soldier in Sierra Leone. I knew that he has now fully recovered through the ceaseless efforts of many kind-hearted people with whom he crossed paths during the hard times of his forced service. After being orphaned and his parents murdered before his eyes by a warlord, he managed to escape just in time after the gory experiences of war.

The words of a stranger, suggesting that he could recreate his destiny through education, changed his life and were the turning point for him. Since graduating from George Washington University in the United States of America, he is now an advocate for peace and child's rights.

Not every boy child soldier's story ends up like this. For many, the ugly head of war never ceases to rear its ugly head. It is well known that exposure to armed conflict is associated with a significantly higher burden of communicable, and non-communicable diseases in children. It is not uncommon to find children dying more from diarrhoea, respiratory infections, malaria, and fever.

Pregnancy and birth in conflict zones is also a substantial risk. Higher rates of teenage pregnancy resulting from rape are typical in these regions, but even in such a chaotic ambience, any hopes of motherhood are quickly dashed by fewer live births, low birth weight, and higher preterm delivery. These observations usually normalise after wars are over or when they are compared with a peaceful control population. This means that many underage girls are in danger and will spend more days out of school, thereby driving further downwards gender inequality.

While things may seem a little grim, the reality is even worse, but it is not one without hope. Most of these children will take a helping hand that is outstretched towards them. They want to be liberated from the curse of war. They want to know peace again. They want to be able to look at the lords of war in their eyes and say "We would not fight the wars for you. If you want honey, then get to the beehives yourself." They want to be able to play football, swim, go to a library or play video games just like they know kids their age are doing. They are willing to close the door to the room of terror and go out into the garden of life. But who will help them?

CHAPTER

6

THE RIGHT TO PLAY

———

"You are worried about seeing him spend his early years in doing nothing. What! Is it nothing to be happy? Nothing to skip, play and run around all day long? Never in his life will he be so busy again."
-Jean Jacques Rousseau

As a child, I cannot think of a more favourite activity that I enjoyed doing than playing throughout the whole day, only pausing to feed, having a bath with little or no rest while my mother worried that I was playing so much. This is not to say that play was the only thing I enjoyed doing with my time as a kid and I am not unique. Starting from very early on in their lives, all children, regardless of what part of the world they are born in, naturally love to play. And they want to get as much of it as they can as long as they are not hungry, having soiled underwear or troubled by their environment.

I have never heard of a child who doesn't love to play. And trust me, I have interacted with a lot of children starting right from my large family of ten siblings to interacting with children as a teacher of basic computing skills to children less than eight years old. I started to think many years ago about why play is so fundamental in the life of a child, and it is a topic that fascinates me till this day. When our family dog whelped and raised her puppies, I noticed that the puppies and their mother were always attached to playing together. This same phenomenon can be observed in virtually almost all mammal species from baboons, lions, zebras, horses and so on. It's the natural language of all living things, and it is so for a reason.

You may be wondering at this point why a book about unveiling tomorrow's genius is mentioning play. Wait! Play! What is so important about it? If you're a neuroscientist or paediatrician, you already have an idea where this is heading. But do you also know that not all children can play in the world for myriad avoidable reasons. You may be imagining at this point that Oche is about to go on one of his long rants about nothing. But please bear with me a little as we together, tease apart this matter of play.

The inventor of the kindergarten, German-born Friedrich Froebel, believed that "play is the highest expression of human development in childhood for it alone is the free expression of what is in the child's soul." It would be unnecessary for me to state here that his ideas for the meaning and importance of play in childhood are blazing across the world today since his conception of it in the 19th century.

He taught that through direct experience with the world, children develop skills to construct an in-depth understanding of their world. He thought holistically about play and believed that aspects like physical development, environment, emotional, social, and spiritual well-being were essential for a child's full development. Shortly after he was born, his mother's health began failing, and resulted in her death when he was only about nine months old. Towards the close of the 18th century, he moved to live with his uncle in

Thuringia, a small town in Germany. I believe that the imperfect stroke of luck he had as a child, and the loss of his mother had a profound influence on his eventual outlook in life and his contribution to the wellbeing of children. Articulating and elaborating certain values as universally true for all children, Froebel developed a set of principles through several of his writings as he worked in Europe in various capacities-as a soldier and in a museum to mention a few.

These principles, developed from his experience and life were curated and published by Professor Tina Bruce in 1987. One of the major things that struck me as I was poring through these principles and studying them was how they spoke to my soul even as an adult. Imagine if we could all agree that childhood is valid in itself and is not a preparation for adulthood, but it is sacrosanct and should be maximised by all humans at that point in their development.

Or that we all believe and practice believing that every child has an inner life, which under favourable conditions materialises everywhere in the world, even in the worst countries where a child can ever be born. Many catastrophes and crises that the human family faces could be avoided with just these two principles. These universal principles are all about emphasising autonomy, intrinsic motivation, and self-directed activity in a child and among groups of children. When they were developed and started becoming popular in Germany, the Prussian government banned his ideas from spreading through a Kindergartenverbot law (German for kindergarten ban).

They considered his thoughts atheistic and capable of breeding anarchy in religion and politics thwarting his raising a butterfly generation. However, any butterfly generation of children are meant to fly into the sunny spring. Teachers from Germany began to spread his ideas across the world and outside Germany due to the draconian edict. Froebel's work has positively affected almost all adults today who have been able to get some form of education or more accurately, "play" at a good kindergarten. To find out more about this unique human being, you can visit the Froebel Trust website at www.froebel.org.uk

Neuroscientists and paediatricians studying child development today tell us that what Froebel outlined is accurate, and they even tell us more by taking it a step further by elucidating the importance of play in childhood. According to neuroscience, play is a state where most adults aspire to be and feel while it is a state of mind where all children should be. The absence of play in a child's life can lead to several neurobiological or psychiatric disorders whether it is absent due to underlying issues in the life of such a child or as a result of the environment the child finds herself in. Because of its importance, the presence or absence of play in a child's life is often even used as a diagnostic criterion by paediatricians in diagnosing some childhood cognitive disabilities.

Play by all standards is necessary for the holistic development of the mammals or in this case, children. According to Professor Steve Siviy and several other psychologists, when juvenile rats are denied the opportunity to play, they become socially, emotionally, and cognitively impaired.[20] The thing is that rats are very similar to humans in their genetic makeup and are usually used in studies that precede human studies and even rarely in cases where it is not possible to study some physical or chemical investigation in humans, one of the choice animals used is usually rats.

It makes sense then that this statement should hold true for any child today. Even parents can observe when they restrict their children from "playing too much" that their child becomes more anxious, and slides into a low mood. It will only take the magic words "you can go out to play now" to lighten up the child's heart. The prefrontal cortex, the part of the brain responsible for complex cognitive behaviour, expression of personality, decision making, and managing social behaviour in mammals undergoes play associated with plasticity, or in order words, new neurons are generated when mammals play.

If Africa is the cradle of humanity, then ancient Greece and its surrounding lands are part of Western civilisation's cradle. Anyone who has watched the movie titled "300" or studied some Greek history would be familiar with the word "Spartan" meaning ascetic and a life bereft of comfort. But even as history popularises the idea of Spartans throwing their weak children to their deaths over the cliff, and the whole population being a functional army, we usually forget to mention that even the Spartans let their children play. Although the only communal mission in the Greek spartan city was to prepare for war, spartan children were still allowed to play by practising wrestling, throwing javelins or discus which were all a form of preparation for the future. Well, do I mean to say we should prepare the children of the world for war today? Absolutely not. But the whole fundamental idea with the spartan's children engaging in these sports was to prepare them for their future reality. Play creates situations that makes children adapt to realities they will encounter in the future in the form of challenges or problems that need to be solved.

Given that the world faces enormous challenges today, there isn't a more accurate time for us to encourage children to go out into nature and play and be happy because their future will be very different from the world we live in today in a whole lot of ways.

Even in Neolithic times, it is possible that children were engaged in a lot of play, but we might never be sure. The toys and drawings in the sand, on trees and splashes in water by prehistoric or Neolithic children, have mostly been lost to nature's eraser, so I would not be candid to say that I am sure children of that era played a lot. But some paintings that have been found in caves which were lower than usual on the wall and smaller in dimension, therefore it might be safe to say that children engaged in some form of enjoyment at that time. Still returning to ancient Greece's story, a significant number of toys in various forms such as clay figures, rattles, horses have been unearthed in this region by archaeologists and were mostly given to children on festivities like the Dionysia or the Anthesteria.[21] To provide an example of such archaeological finds, there lies a cup in the Louvre Museum in Paris on which a young man is depicted standing on his left leg and holding a goblet in what is interpreted as someone performing balancing exercises. The Mediterranean from historical times and even today have always been a migration hotspot and melting pot uniting different cultures of the human race- Arabs, Romans, Berbers, and Carthaginians meaning that the artefacts found in this region which can attest to the universality of play among the human family and especially among its youngest ones.

In contemporary times, we know that play is an essential component of childhood. It is common knowledge among experts who deal with children that play is vital for healthy brain development that manifests in a child's life through emotional, cognitive, and social balance in how kids carry out their activities and solve problems. Even parents are not left out of the loop of observation. Many parents can attest to this, and many visits to the paediatrician with a far too solemn child often are rewarded with the simple advice to create opportunities for the downcast child to play more. And you can bet that most paediatricians are good at playing with children. That is the first thing they try to do with each child who visits their practice even if it is for a case of troublesome diarrhoea. Play speaks to a child's mind so much that they often connect easily with people who can establish a play ritual with them. It goes without saying that while playing with other children or adults, children learn to master their world and develop some critical skills like negotiation and resilience needed to conquer their world. They also learn skills like sharing, assertiveness, and conflict resolution.

I have always wanted to investigate Adolf Hitler's childhood because I believe that his childhood must have been bereft of play and given his unpopular antics that lead to one of the most catastrophic events in human history. If you know about his childhood, I would really love to hear from you. I would be really grateful to hear from you because we have to solve the puzzle together. Ever played Peek-a-boo with a baby before? Or even simply exchanged the furtive smiles? I'm sure if you could remember well, the baby did not want you to stop. That is the hardwiring for play that I was referring to that starts in childhood.

"But aren't children playing already?" you may be asking yourself. Well, the handwriting on the wall points to the fact that many children are not playing as much as they should and for those kids who have the opportunity to play, they cannot participate in active play. Because of the almost universal consensus that play is important in children's lives, The United Nations Convention on the Rights of the Child made sure to capture this in the binding agreement that most nations have ratified today making it the world's most ratified human right's treaty.

This document says "…every child has the right to rest and leisure, to engage in play and recreational activities appropriate to the age of the child and to participate freely in cultural life and the arts. That member governments shall respect and promote the right of the child to participate fully in cultural and artistic life and shall encourage the provision of appropriate and equal opportunities for cultural, artistic, recreational and leisure activity."[22]

Unfortunately, the peaceful and alluring call of the wild in childhood for many children is threatened, and the idea of play has been completely erased from the family and social constructs especially in low and middle-income countries such as in many African countries, as well as in some South-Asian countries like Bangladesh. For these African children, the sanctuary of play has been desecrated by never-ending violence in their communities, child labour or in some cases due to the poor handling of childhood disabilities by the incompetent or rigid hearted governments and stakeholders in these countries.

Environmental degradation also threatens play both in childhood and youth in its entirety, as we would see in chapter nine later. I still remember how my father called me up one day to the balcony of our house in 2001 to listen to the sound of gunshots coming from a distance, this was during a violent religious riot in Jos, Nigeria between Christians, and Muslims. My father explained to me that our city had changed that day and would never be the same again.

The evenings when I would go to our back garden to play football with my friends on the grounds of a vineyard my father planted seemed to be over. Among my friends at the time were both Muslim and Christian children. But everyone felt the pulsating tension in the town, and it was difficult to trust anyone as soon as the first gun was fired at the beginning of the religious crisis. It was not that we children had any qualms with playing with each other, but our parents would no longer allow us to go to the neighbours' houses because they were of a different religion and if our parents were not scared of the Muslim neighbours smashing our heads on a wall, the parents of our Muslim friends were scared that their children would be poisoned by Christian families if they allowed them to visit. This was how I got my first taste of how community violence can completely disrupt childhood. This is not to say that I compared myself to children who were forced to take combatant roles in conflicts. However, I know that I began to hate every form of violence in which adults were involved. Children are the ones who suffer the most in these conflicts, no matter how you look at it. As an African proverb says, 'when two elephants fight, it is the ground that suffers it'.

According to the international non-governmental organisation, Save the Children, one in four African children live in a conflict zone and in 2018 alone, almost 1500 children were maimed by armed forces in as little as six African countries.[22] If you think of every time you have had to ignore the news when you turn on your television of new sprouting violence and conflict in another African country, and calculate the number of children's lives that are affected by all these mushrooming conflicts and instability due to terrorism, civil war and the struggle for finite natural resources and political power, you might begin to appreciate the magnitude of the problem that we are dealing with. For each child who lives in a violent community, this means that the child's mental health is put to the test by the toxic environment in which she would have to continue living with her family. And even when they must flee conflict, new migration-related problems that have to do with settling and integrating into a new community continue to deny such a child the chance to play and learn about the world through play.

To appreciate the magnitude of the problem and possibly decide to change the status quo as an adult, you would have to decide and make up your mind about your views on the nature and value of play. Are you someone who just ignores it? Or maybe you are the type who considers it a pure waste of time. Some adults might also think that play is dangerous, and they always panic when children play. Others, however, view it as a necessary tool that helps a child to socialise and at least learn something about their immediate environment and the structure of the society around them. I beg you to belong to the latter group because that is where the future of humanity lies.

With the changing complexity and the widening span of war zones, children are significantly impacted by conflict, and the possibility for children to enjoy their childhood through play is under threat. Schools which were formerly safe havens and protected from the impacts of disputes are often attacked by warring parties in low and middle-income countries where violence is common in various forms. Children are also attacked or kidnapped on their way to and from school. These kinds of attacks violate the Geneva convention as well as other treaties protecting children.

The lords of war do not seem to care since justice is rarely served hot and swiftly. In some conflict zones such as Syria, Yemen, and Iraq, it is not uncommon to hear that a child picked up an unexploded bomb which then explodes while the child who thought it was a new toy was playing with it. In these countries, the most common form of injury affecting children is gunshot wounds and injuries resulting from the impact of pieces of shrapnel piercing through the body. Burns and trauma of the head and neck are also ubiquitous. Sadly, boys and girls also experience sexual exploitation, and violence in the form of rape which puts them in danger of contracting sexually transmitted infections like gonorrhoea, and syphilis to mention but a few. How can a child think of play in such conditions? Most children who live in countries where these kinds of events occur are usually confused and find it difficult to dream of the future let alone play with their friends. Some of the brave ones still find a way to play even amid the war around them.

I still remember some years ago, while studying to become an epidemiologist, staff from the International Committee of the Red Cross visited our university in France. They gave a very captivating talk on the need to respect the Geneva convention in conflict and how warring parties might be made to appreciate it.

One interesting thing I picked up that day was how armed conflicts could create environmental hazards that threaten children's play long after a conflict has ended. Landmines and unexploded bombs or rockets continue to be dangerous to children long after the war has ended. In Afghanistan, Nepal, and Eritrea, more than half of the injuries that resulted from the late explosion of these ordinances occurred to children. Children are also very susceptible to chemical agents which are sometimes used in conflicts due to their small body size, and higher respiratory rate.

After the 20-year conflict between the United States of America and Vietnam ended in 1975 with President Nixon declaring that, "peace with honour" had been achieved, what lay behind as the curtains were closed on the conflict would continue to have impacts on the lives of children for many decades. Agent Orange, an herbicide, was seriously employed by the USA in its chemical warfare program. Almost 4 million Vietnamese were exposed to this chemical during the war as the US struggled to decimate the indefatigable Vietnamese warriors and citizens.

Over the years, doctors in Vietnam began to observe strange birth defects in children which prevented them from leading a completely normal childhood. Scientific studies were launched to investigate the strange phenomenon. Some scientists claimed it was due to hereditary transfer of Agent Orange defects while others disagreed and thought it was probably some other genetic factor. The disagreement on the actual cause of these birth defects has remained in debate for decades, but in 2006, some scientists summarised and compared the evidence from as far back as 1966. Guess what they found? Agent Orange is responsible for the increased cases of birth defects in Vietnamese children.[24] Not surprising if you ask me.

Poisoning caused by heavy metal lead is common in children who play in the dirt and at abandoned gold mining sites in Zamfara State located in Northwest Nigeria and other African countries. Lead is usually used in the artisanal process of mining gold, and the toxic metal percolates the soil and water that gathers in the ditch which children who either must work or play in such areas come in contact with this dangerous chemical. Lead also penetrates children's bodies when they live in houses painted with lead-based paint.

High levels of lead poisoning attack the brain and central nervous system leading to coma or convulsions in children. Children who have been affected by high-level lead poisoning are at the risk of suffering from developmental problems like behavioural issues and mental retardation. Even at low levels of concentration in a child's body, lead can impact brain development by reducing the child's intelligence quotient (IQ). That is not all sadly. Low levels of lead can also cause increased antisocial behaviour, which directly impacts children's ability to play. It can also lead to reduced attention span in children which, together with the low IQ can significantly affect the child's ability to attend school, make progress academically and socialise with friends at school.

When there is an outbreak of lead poisoning in a place like Zamfara, experts often make suggestions, and they try to remove lead from the environment before children can be treated. This is, however, very difficult. It usually involves removing all contaminated soil in the village and replacing it with fresh, clean soil. As you can imagine, this process is costly and is hardly ever done in the affected Nigerian State. This means that treatment is delayed and because it is not safe to play outside or even breathe, children have to live without dreaming of playing because their parents become cautious of letting them play outside.

It makes life look like a little natural gulag where even your environment becomes your prison, and that is how I imagine these children and their parents must feel with such an environmental hazard. While play is the only language children understand, no child can play safely in an environment like that. It is even worse when children have to work in gold mining sites to support their families instead of playing to improve their creativity and attending school.

Around the globe, 152 million children-both boys and girls are currently subjected to child labour which comes in many forms and is executed differently. Children may be forced to work in mining sites, livestock herding (as is common with the Fulani ethnic group in Nigeria), tending to farmlands, serving as domestic household maids or servant boys, or performing duties in factories, this is common with children in Bangladesh and Cambodia. This illegal child labour industry generates about 150 billion dollars a year. While armed conflicts threaten children's ability to play safely, it is also associated with child labour. Child labour is higher in countries affected by armed conflict, especially for dangerous work.

Unicef, one of the organisations at the forefront of the fight for children's well-being, states that child labour is harmful to a child's physical, mental, social, and moral development.

Child labour is driven by poverty and economic calamity. Kids from poorer households are at an increased risk of being poached for work to contribute some income to their families. However, the problem is that many of them, through the various jobs they take up, put themselves in danger either physically or mentally that affects their ability to participate in and enjoy playing with other children to improve their creativity. They simply are forced to grow up too fast, and the door to the wonderland of childhood is shut on them without mercy. While they participate in child labour instead of having a normal childhood, children undergo multiple cycles of poverty and abuse, contrasting with any inkling of dignity left that the human species possesses.

We simply cannot continue to deny the young and vulnerable members of our species the very tools they need to equip themselves for the future because we want to make big profits through cheap labour. You may think that you have nothing to do with it, but we are all guilty. Most of the chocolate you eat or the coffee you drink is produced through child labour and exploitation of vulnerable people by big companies seated in the northern hemisphere. The effects of globalisation which has resulted in larger industries being located far away from residential areas remove children from the environment where play is possible thereby threatening children's right to play correlating with countries and communities having high rates of child labour.

The eighth Sustainable Development Goal (SDG) set by the international community is based on an article of the Convention on the Rights of the Child, requiring governments to protect children from harmful and exploitative activities. This SDG underscores the commitment to eliminate child labour in the world. This is a noble goal in which all of us can be actors, role players and enablers who work in concert towards its realisation. The stakes are high. Children who lose their childhood to child labour become troublesome adults who can become menaces in the society, and the sad thing is that at that point, they can hardly be steered in the right direction. It is easier to bend a green stick than a dry one. The dry stick gets broken.

As I mentioned earlier, one other factor that seems to threaten play in childhood is disability. Disability, although a severe challenge in the lives of many children in the world, is not a factor that totally annihilates the capacity to play and enjoy life at least to a certain extent. Around 150 million children live with disabilities globally, and in the developing countries of the world, the data is not even well collated, so this figure may underestimate the reality of the situation on ground.

Normal children often engage in solitary and communal or social play, which is characterised by language, movement, and role-play. Disabled children, on the other hand, may find it difficult to engage in either some forms of play or in any kind of play at all. For example, children with Autism Spectrum Disorder, have speech and communication impediments, this defect make them have stereotypical behaviour. This sort of behaviour makes it difficult for them to interact and play with other children who also find it difficult to break through a seemingly high wall of defence that guards these children's hearts with autism. Autism can also affect posture and the way a child moves.

This is a limitation on the range of play activities such a child can attempt without proper therapy and support. Children with forms of blindness or cerebral palsy might have problems with spatial orientation while their tactile senses develop in the case of visual impairment or problems with locomotion. These all threatens a child's ability to explore his environment and learn the critical survival lessons that nature tries to teach all of us from a tender age.

The good news is that there is substantial evidence that even when a child is severely disabled, he can still engage in some or all forms of play in the dawn of early childhood. It is imperative for all of us to hold our governments accountable because as signatories to the United Nations Convention on the Rights of the Child, they have a duty to ensure that children with a disability receive special care and support that would enable them to engage in self-initiated play while taking into account the limitations of the condition that makes them disabled. It is often only when you look around that you realise that this problem is far-reaching in society. If each of us decides to take action in the little corners of the world where we wield influence, we can get all children playing and fulfilling the call of the wild wonderland of childhood.

Beyond the moral obligation that hangs in our hearts as humans, and the facts supporting the facilitation of play in childhood for all children of the world but especially in regions of the world where they are denied this privilege such as in Africa and in some parts of Asia, we should also consider the perspective that play in childhood is a human right enshrined in the Convention on the Rights of the Child ratified by almost all nations.

Parties to the treaty recognise and guarantee the child's right to rest and leisure, engage in play and recreational activities appropriate to the age of the child, and participate freely in cultural life and the arts of the community they are found in and of the world. This is impressive to start with if you ask me. But several nuances have prevented the fruits of such noble and universal agreements to positively change the lives of many children in Africa and the rest of the world. But we can do something about it because whatever the human spirit sets out to accomplish is undoubtedly accomplished now or later.

It is inaccurate to view 'survival' in a child as the mere effort to maintain biological and physiological processes in the present and ensure its continuity into the future. Because children's play can be considered a means to enhance adaptive capabilities and resilience, we should also learn to appreciate its contribution to health and overall well-being and strength[25]. Play is also a form of participation in life by children interwoven into everyday life. Therefore, denying children the right to play is the same as denying them the right to live and thrive. One aspect of the right to play worth discussing is the availability of facilities for play.

Who is responsible for providing facilities that children could use to enjoy their right to play? When cities are constructed, or children attend schools that either do not have facilities that enable play or have unsafe play paraphernalia, who is to blame? Children's need for facilities like space and time to allow for play is often ignored in policy formulation by governments and private individuals when planning or executing projects and in policy implementation. This could result in a decline of emotional, physical, social, and cognitive ability in children not because they do not want to play as nature demands them to, but because society has made it impossible for them to participate in everyday life by playing.

Because of the importance of play in the lives of children and also due to the consequences of its absence and the fact that it is not a luxury but a right that comes along with other basic necessities like survival and safety, we must ensure that we perform our roles towards making it a material experience for all the children of the world. In your little sphere of influence, you can create awareness of the importance of play in childhood, promote it and protect the conditions that guarantee this inalienable right. While creating the awareness of this right may be obvious and involve little actions like respecting this right and creating opportunities for our children to play, we can accomplish this by merely ensuring that the conditions are right for children to play. This aspect is crucial because the right to play is often overlooked and ignored as unimportant.

One known fact in public health, for example, is that the availability of green parks is usually associated with healthier lifestyles, better overall health in adults and in children. The provision of green spaces would ensure that children not only enjoy play more but that their brains and cognitive processes develop holistically in line with recent evidence that contact with green spaces in children is associated with improved mental and physical health.[26] Children also need to be protected from all forms of child abuse, cruel acts, neglect, and exploitation always and while they play even in times of war or conflict. Therefore, there is a need to create safe playing spaces for children like parks while ensuring that the structural engineering of residences is designed to support play and freedom.

Whatever direction the world may go, we must harness the power of play to unite children and show them the marvels of the world. With play, we can build a generation of children who are resilient, strong, courageous, intelligent, and ready for the future in the face of the never-ending wars, diseases, and violence that confront them as they grow into adulthood. Because play also builds independence, children who play will be equipped to create a bright future for themselves and their families. Let us all do what we can to get children on the fields, in the playgrounds, and in school speaking the language they know best-laughter shared with their friends, sweet fatigue from running around and deep joy from playing.

CHAPTER

7

LITTLE DROWNING VOICES IN A WORLD THAT WON'T STOP IMPALING GAY PEOPLE

"Children are not things to be moulded but are people to be unfolded."
-Jess Lair

One of the indisputable natural facts of life is that we cannot choose a child's sexual identity. This statement is bound to send chills down the spines of many Africans and some conservative Westerners, Middle-Easterners and Asians. But I will also add to their discomfort, not out of schadenfreude or vitriol that we also cannot determine what gender a child will identify with as an adult. Yes, it is true that society and the family norms we were raised in can play a role in shaping who we are and, in these cases, presented above, stifle, or promote these tendencies in a child who would one day grow up to be an adult. What humans for many generations or in different societies have not thought of however is what the consequences of putting people into an identity straitjacket will have on the individual and on the expanse of humanity as he or she interacts with other humans as one who has never really discovered a very valid and complete part of themselves.

The product of this millennial practice bludgeoning the minds of children into a path right from their tender age into a sexual fantasy that mismatches their biology and real-life aspirations buried deep within results in dysfunctional adults who are not able to express themselves fully. Remember, this is the 21st century, and most countries in the world somewhat practice a semblance of democracy. Now, here is what I think. If we live in the human rights era and humans, starting from their childhood, are still bullied by society to live a life that is also a shadow of what they are really built for, aren't we merely promoting the biggest irony of all time? We have succeeded in sending a man to the moon, landing a probe on a comet moving at blinding velocity and achieving peace gradually through fewer conflicts than in previous ages, eradicated smallpox and are at the cusp of sending poliomyelitis on the same final journey. Still, we have individuals living in skins that do not belong to them and acting in ways that they never would have acted in an ulterior scenario and in an alternate reality much to their excruciating discomfort and deeply moving unhappiness. Would our ancestors really wish they lived to see our day, or would they cringe at the thought of how we pretend to be free-living agents? If you think of it, the chaos this unravels within the human family is unfathomable. Before you wonder why I have mentioned our ancestors, let's go on a journey back in time and probe homosexuality from a few steps down the historical staircase.

Today, most modern humans are aware that we had hunter-gatherer ancestors who lived by foraging and sleeping most of the day without tasking their body beyond that which was necessary for performing the basics of life's needs-Food, sex, and shelter which they found on trees and in natural caves. I am referring to our shared ancestors who walked the Earth about 200 000 years ago. They have left us several relics that include a highly active amygdala; the brain's region that guides our fear response. This ensured that they didn't take any uncalculated risks while in the Savannah to avoid being mauled by lions or bitten by poisonous serpents. It made them rise to challenges to defend themselves from troublesome and warring human tribes who threatened their survival. What puzzles me though as someone without a training in anthropology or evolutionary biology is why they left us such an heirloom- a highly active amygdala. Although we live in tremendously safer societies now, our danger instinct is still as active as that of our human ancestors. You may be wondering why I have suddenly switched gear to talk about an evolutionary concept rather than on sexuality as I had initially commenced. Well, the reason is that I want to use that single example handpicked from potentially hundreds of thousands of evolutionary heirlooms to make a simple point that is the crux of debates across many societies worldwide today and may continue to be so for a while.

I was surfing the internet one evening in the spring of 2011, and I was not prepared for what appeared on my computer screen. Archaeologists had unearthed some ancient human remains again; this was what I had read that rainy evening. I was startled but excited because the article claimed that the man may have been gay. Still, the archaeologists were not really sure[27] Even though he had died 5000 years earlier, the archaeologists were convinced that the way he was buried with his head facing eastwards and surrounded by what seemed to be household items or for simplicity, kitchenware suggested that he was probably of a different sexual orientation than was common at the time. For several skeletons unearthed in the Czech Republic and most times around the world, males were usually buried with weapons and materials that showed strength and domination rather than effeminate objects such as was found in this prehistoric grave.

Men were also traditionally buried with the head lying westward rather than eastward in the region of this finding in the Czech Republic. In fact, this man was buried precisely how women were laid to rest at that time-with pots and no gender-specific paraphernalia or weaponry denoting masculinity according to the rites of the Corded-ware culture of antiquity. The lead researcher of the team who made the findings, Kamila Remisova Vesinova was sure that it was not a mistake because burial rites were a thing of immense importance during the era the man was alive.

I was befuddled with this finding. since I had by that time become very interested in learning about our evolutionary past. I knew that this was something significant, but I could not understand the discovery's implications at the time. To me, it meant two things. It either suggested this man was queer or that he was possibly a transgender. This went against the grain of thought in 2011, at least in Nigeria where I was at the time, the standard narrative was that queerness was a western agenda to make the black race effeminate and emasculate them. Some others thought that the practice was introduced on the African continent by Islamic slave traders.[28] It was also widely believed that it was a modern trend that had come upon the world from which parents and societies must protect their teenage children at all costs as if it was a highly lethal and contagious disease. This is not surprising mainly because Africans have a rich cultural heritage which they often like to protect with taboos, superstition, frightening mythical tales and sometimes violence, because it's a traditional based society.

Same-sex relationships, however, are not alien neither is it a recent occurrence in sub-Saharan Africa as many religious or conservative thinking people would have themselves believe. The widely held assertions by many Africans that queerness is not part of their historical heritage comes with the social consequence of the dangerous stigmatisation and many times brutal attack on their kinsfolk who engage in same-sex activities, harbour an inkling, or be perceived by the society to do so as well as those struggling with different sexual identities than is common with denizens of a given community like in Lagos for instance.

When European explorers like Sir Richard Burton and Mungo Park visited Sub-Saharan Africa, what they did not realise at first was that most of the recorded history that we have on the continent was unavailable in written form and the onus would fall on explorers like them to give accounts. History in Africa was passed down in a different form than was the norm in Europe through oral means from elders to children in tales, poetry, and folklore in most of these regions for a very long time.

Emanating from the 19th century or some little time beyond that, various written literature can be found that are replete with stories of male and female homosexuality and same-sex marriages that span from the north in Sudan to southern Africa and from Kenya to the West in Nigeria and Benin republic. There is no scarcity of love stories between women or between men, and this all happened before the arrival of European civilisation or to put it in a different way, the colonial masters met Africans already having these practices long before they could influence them as many ignorantly claim.

Homosexual practices in Ethiopia were not uncommon among the Semitic Hashiri, the Galla and Somali tribes. Richard Burton noted socio-cultural aspects of some West-African societies are favourable and respectful of people's sexual predilections. Although many of my kinsmen will argue and chastise anyone for telling them to allow people to develop sexually into the identity that they choose and that best fits them even if they display these tendencies from childhood. Few of my kinsmen will be able to offer any words more valid than the ones below to counter an empathy call on their conscience:

"Gender has very little to do with anatomy.... The Earth is looked at, from my tribal perspective, as a very, very delicate machine or consciousness, with high vibrational points, which certain people must be guardians of in order for the tribe to keep its continuity with the gods and with the spirits that dwell there-- spirits of this world and spirits of the other world. Any person who is linked between this world and the other world experiences a state of vibrational consciousness which is far higher, and far different, from the one that a normal person would experience. This is what makes a gay person gay. This kind of function is not one that society votes for certain people to fulfil. It is one that people are said to decide on prior to being born. You decide that you will be a gatekeeper before you are born. And it is that decision that provides you with the equipment that you bring into this world. So, when you arrive here, you begin to vibrate in a way that Elders can detect as meaning that you are connected with a gateway somewhere"[29]

These words are not mine but are sacredly held beliefs by the Dagara tribe somewhere in Burkina Faso which is a West African country like Nigeria and Ghana and this way of thinking dates from very far back in our regional collective anthropological history. So, are we really a nation of people who then respect the wisdom of the ancestors? You tell me. In January 2014, three years after that spring evening when I read about the story of "Czech gay caveman archeological discovery", Nigeria's former President Goodluck Jonathan signed a draconian law criminalising same-sex relationships, raising several questions in my mind.

How would a teenager who through the lottery of birth was born in Nigeria and through no fault of hers discovered that her future romantic partnerships would only have meaning with someone who is precisely in the same form as she was biologically forged go on in life? Was she sentenced to a life of denial and physical and mental chastisement by the government that should protect her livelihood and maintain a society for her to pursue happiness?

While many still argue that colonialists spread homosexuality in Africa, the law signed by the Nigerian former president was a buildup on old British Laws that stipulated that gay relationships were outlawed. The law only served to empower law enforcement officers to abuse not just the rights of anyone who is queer or is suspected to be, it made them feel like they could physically torture and detain people as they liked. By the way, the draconian penalty for being gay in Nigeria is a 14-year sentence in jail. The reception of the law by the society was even more disastrous.

To be fair, Nigeria has never really had the best human rights records, nor could it be said that people live relatively in harmony with each other all the time without some form of chaos looming around the corner. To be honest, as a Nigerian, I always have a part of my heart reserved for turmoil. It's just like emotional insurance you take out, only this time, the premium you pay is a heightened sense of fear and situational awareness. The thing is that the law also had an extremely negative spin-off on Nigerians. Many do not wait on the government to mete out "justice" to these discriminated individuals. They still usually take the law into their hands. In the months following the passage of the law, Nigeria recorded a significant increase in the number of mob attacks on queer or transgender individuals and on Human rights defenders who act to assert the rights of the gay community in the country.[30] Now the question that begs for answer is how is a teenage child who has discovered that he is gay supposed to react to all these? Can they really grow and generally develop into fully functional adults who can contribute positively to national development without being cut short by bludgeoning death from a mob or imprisonment? Isn't this a betrayal of trust by the Nigerian government to members of their small West African patch of land? I cannot begin to think of the mental anguish that many have to go through in questioning if they are "normal" humans because of a slight difference in sexual affinity.

There is a somewhat redundant problem-solving technique that is very common to many Africans that is akin to cleaning a wound with dirt, and I don't know if it is worse in Nigeria, but it seems so to me. When someone is involved in an accident that results in a fractured limb, they go to the local bone setters instead of an orthopaedic surgeon. When they feel feverish, they go to the local traditional healer for a herb and root concoction. Little wonder the most popular coronavirus remedy at the dawn of the 2019 global Covid-19 pandemic most Nigerians thought about was the Madagascan potion that is clinically unproven, but since it's "unorthodox", they demanded it (these are all debatable of course).

However, it was later proven that the claim by Madagascan authorities that the herbal potion provided immunity against the dreaded Covid-19 virus was a hoax. That is why parents with children who develop psychological problems like Attention Deficit Hyperactivity Disorder (ADHD), depression, and violent behaviour would quickly head off to their Pastor or Priest rather than seek the services of a trained mental health professional or neuroscientist. This is no different for their teenagers who they suspect to be queer.

Today, many children are subjected to various forms of deprivations and extreme inconvenience through conversion therapies that aim to "normalise" their sexual preferences at the hands of people who claim to speak the voice of God forgetting that beard's do not grow in heaven. The entire span of these therapies ranges from seemingly harmless prayers to extreme practices like fasting without food or water. They are held for days in conversion centres such as the Islamic rehabilitation centre I mentioned earlier. Indeed, some children were sent there because they were suspected to be gay, and the parents thought the kindest thing to do to a loved one was to send them to that Gulag rather than report to the Nigerian authorities who could impose stricter measures. Sometimes, gay teenagers and young adults become vulnerable to sexual violence from people who blackmail them with the fact of their orientation and start an abusive rape relationship where the victim is not willing to report the case for fear of being exposed as gay.

[30]In their minds and in what calls for empathy from any well-meaning person, the consequences are much more severe. I don't mean that I agree. My point is that no one should be forced to choose between two challenging places. Whenever I think of these happenings, all I am sure of is that the parents and society will always act better if they are convinced with ethical arguments and a good reason to respect everyone's rights whether they are teenagers or young adults.

I first came in contact with Edwin Adenuga in 2019. Some of his tweets sifted into my feed when a mutual friend had liked and shared them. The tweets were strongly worded and did not contain fear, but despair could be felt from the author's heart. He was voicing deeply held emotions and pain that resulted from persecution that he endured as a gay young fella living in Nigeria. Naturally, this got my interest because I am moved deeply when minorities are persecuted anywhere in the world. Sometimes, I can do something about it by raising awareness at conferences through presentations or protesting, other times, I am completely paralysed with the inability to do anything, which makes my heart sink to the ground where no human should tread upon. I was in the metro in Paris when I saw his tweets and swiftly made a mental note to contact Edwin as soon as I reached my destination. The stories that he recounted to me afterwards when I called him are what I would share with you below, and I would allow you to be the judge yourself on whether there is justice in the persecution of minorities.

Since he was a child, Edwin had always known he was different. He would play with barbie dolls, mostly with the little girls in his neighbourhood in the small ghetto town of Ajegunle in Lagos. As a result, he was always bullied in school and at home by more macho driven boys who thought he was odd. His complaints to his parents fell on deaf ears as they were busy trying to survive the economic hardships and didn't believe that anything was wrong with their son being bullied at school. According to him, the trend continued until his teenage years when his friends started having sexual relationships with their classmates, but he couldn't feel any attraction towards females. The male body fascinated him, and that was where he thought he would satisfy his passion. He met an older male partner some years down the line, and a blossoming relationship unfolded between them. He could not hide his joy as he exuded strong confidence.

He had found love in his life at last, and things began to make sense to him. One day, his older friend created a Facebook post which depicted them sharing a romantic moment together, this led to a cascade of events snowballing into a lot of despair and discomfort in his life. His sisters informed their parents about the post and the parents arranged an appointment between him and a catholic priest for spiritual cleansing because they were convinced beyond doubt that their son was possessed by a promiscuous spirit that would lead him to destruction and condemnation by God.

The priest questioned Edwin on whether he had had any sexual relationship with men before, Edwin decided not to respond as according to him such a question was intruding into his privacy. The priest would not have any of that and kept rewording the problem in different forms.

"Do you like boys?" "Has a man touched you before my son?' When he realised that the interrogation was not heading anywhere, he choked Edwin's neck with one hand and started repeatedly punching him on the face with the other hand until he got tired, and blood was flowing from the poor boy's nostrils. He quickly apologised for the short temper and asked him to say some Hail Mary's for one week and, that he would see him after that. Edwin has been called girly by his professors who mock him during class for his effeminate attributes, and one professor told him that he was disgusted by him and ashamed to be his professor even though he thought he was an intelligent student.

How is a young lad supposed to grow "spiritually" or learn under these conditions? More recently, while he was on his way back from the library, a group of men started calling him names to deride him which he ignored. When they realised that they couldn't get his attention, they surrounded him and threw rocks at him while some of them hit him with batons of wood on his head. Today, his body is covered with several ugly old scars from incidents like these. The good thing I noticed from my conversations with him is his calm and cheerful countenance. He believes that despite these challenges, his future would be beautiful.

However, he still doesn't think that he would survive for long in Nigeria with the way things are going over there. He explained with much concern that living there would be living in paranoia since you never know if you would live to see the next few moments of life just for having a different sexual orientation from what society thinks is normal.

This is made worse in Nigeria especially when you do not have any form of social or financial capital to make you a prince or princess in your country folks' hearts. All these put a strain on his mental and physical wellbeing. I fought to hide the tears that were welling up in my eyes and the emotion in my voice as we talked on the video call while he shared his stories. His dream is to have a good life with a man he loves.

His parents also joined the band of people who persecute him by threatening to disown him. Although he decided to leave the nest, moving out of his parent's house made him more vulnerable to persecutions at a young age.

There are worse stories than this in Nigeria or Africa with people being tortured and burnt to death with rubber tyres hung around their necks. Being a queer is no easy feat in Nigeria. I have lived in Europe for over half a decade, and I have several friends who are queer. The experience they have is usually positive even though there are exceptions. No one in the 21st century will burn a gay French man alive with the French government's full support. Such things are practices of the dark ages, and they remain behind those shameful curtains of history.

For example, my French friend Henri, who has been openly gay since his teenage years has received support from his family since he came out open to them. He finds it difficult to understand how people can be discriminated against for something as necessary as sexual orientation. He did not have any professor make him leave the class in university, nor is he prohibited from holding public office for being gay. Why do these things only happen in the developing world? Is there a link to economic hardship or technological disadvantages? These and many more are questions that the social sciences would have to answer if any positive changes to Africa's human rights record are to be made.

Many well-meaning Africans and indeed Nigerians take inspiration from their religious holy books as the fuel that drives their oppression of queer individuals. And the idea that a child could one day develop, and practice same-sex relationships is something that many religious people would hardly ever accept especially in Africa, and many fear for several reasons, including being ostracised from their families and religious communities. It might be necessary to take a small detour into the roads that lead to this kind of unprogressive thinking patterns which are simply like using donkeys to travel in New York today.

The church and mosque wield a significant influence in the lives of billions of people across the world and have done so for centuries. The thing to know about this is that it is not necessarily a wonderful thing for humanity because people surrender their critical thinking on the altar where the clergy speak or on the ground where their faces kiss the Earth. It is really infuriating when you think about it: and when it comes to the issue of queerness, it is challenging to communicate rationally with individuals who have chosen to make organised religion the only thing that matters in their lives without thinking about life's most profound questions themselves. Actually, the reality is that life evolves and as the universe changes even though everything looks the same, so must we. We must be able to mull over an idea. Turn it over and over again and debate it to a logical conclusion rather than flaring up in wild feats of tantrums like a kid who has been denied candies by his mother.

In 1895, the iconic Irish writer Oscar Wilde was charged, and accused of sodomy after an associate left a card with inscriptions denoting that he was gay.[31] After a series of legal battles by Oscar's lawyer to save his neck, still he was jailed. He was first sent to the Newgate prison in London, and subsequently to Pentonville prison, where he had to participate in hard labour, which consisted of walking for many hours on a treadmill and separating fibres within old navy ropes. In this prison, he was permitted to only read the Bible and the Pilgrim's Progress, an allegory of salvation written by John Bunyan. But the events that set the stage for Oscar Wilde's incarceration and isolation from the world preceded the British legal system of the 19th century. The truth is that homophobia and the whole pariah associated with it has some Judeo-Christian origins.

Previously, Jews (Hebrews) did not regard the practice of homosexuality as a moral decadence that needed a holy sanction. Any student of Jewish history can deduce that the temples of Jews and Canaanites used homosexual prostitutes to perform some of their sacred rituals.

However, it happened that during the Jewish nationalism, the Jews decided to do away with many of their cultural norms and adopt new ones. You can guess by now that homosexuality was one of the demonised norms said to be ungodly. This can also be attributed to the fact that the early Jewish tribes were small and surrounded by stronger and larger hostile neighbours. The need for a healthy and sizeable Jewish population probably motivated them to frown on non-reproductive sexual acts such as homosexuality, birth control and other sexually stimulating activities which were not geared towards reproduction intending to protect their survival.[32] Homosexuality would later be viewed in their society, in the same light as idolatry which carried the death penalty.

The Judeo-Christian view breeds a form of sexual anxiety and was recognised as a pathology in the medical journals even early in this century. At least I can speak for myself even though I do not qualify to make a direct comparison since I am not gay, my first sexual experience was chaotic because I had thought that I would be struck dead on the spot for committing a grave sin. In the end, my first experience was ruined. I know that many people have similar tales or even worse than that because even for me who had never taken religion too seriously, it seemed to pose a problem.

The loss of the concept of sin by Judeo-Christian juggernauts across the world as science prevailed, did not leave human society unscathed. Sin was replaced by medical experts making a diagnosis of homosexuality as a pathology that required medical attention. A lot of medical papers were written about it, and I am sure that many conferences followed.

Thankfully for humanity, a UCLA psychologist Evelyn Hooker performed a ground-breaking study that changed the face of the psychopathological judgement of homosexuals. At that time in the 1950s when she conducted the study, the prevailing medical mantra regarding the claimed pathology of homosexuality was that; "when such homosexual behaviour persists in an adult, it is then a symptom of a severe emotional disorder." Hooker designed her experiment by selecting 30 homosexuals who were healthy and not undergoing any treatment and matched them with 30 heterosexuals of similar age, IQ, education, and socioeconomic status. She obtained information on life histories and put them through a series of psychological tests. When the results were ready, they were analysed by experts who were blinded, that is, they didn't know if the results they were analysing were from the subjects who were homosexuals or heterosexuals.[33] It was simply impossible to do so. Hooker reached the glaring conclusion that there was no connection between homosexual orientation and emotional disturbance. In fact, to put it bluntly, science confirmed that homosexuality was not pathological. It was not a disease. Since she made this paradigm-shifting discovery, this study has been replicated in labs worldwide with similar results. What else do you want?

On our high cosmic horse, we often forget that as humans, we are still just mere animals given to the whims of our primitive brains and the chemistry that takes place in it. When a pharmaceutical company wants to develop medicines, vaccines and other therapeutic agents for human consumption, the initial conception and design of such a project are done with animals because although not all observations made in animal models hold true in humans, they give us clues on how such therapeutic agents will behave in humans. What I mean is that, even if our paths diverged from our evolutionary history, we still share a huge part of the basic essence of being with other animal species. To put in the spotlight some scientific facts, humans share about 97.5% of their genes with mice, 98.7% with Bonobos, 99% with Chimpanzees. Humans even share 60% of genes with the banana that is eaten at breakfast! We are all connected. Should we be so different in our behaviour then? But we are at least in our ability to use and make tools, in our quest and appreciation of spirituality and our ability to create and function in an intersubjective reality.[34]

In his excellent book Gay, straight, and the reason why, Simon Levay makes an argument for the natural occurrence of homosexuality by taking readers on a journey through evolution, anatomy and endocrinology asserting reasons why some humans are gay while others aren't by using the term gender-nonconformist.[35] Gender-nonconformity is simply what we observe when an individual behaves in a way that does not match the expected masculine or feminine gender norms. Citing several examples using the presence or absence of the hormone called testosterone, Levay made a strong argument for how gender-nonconformity may arise through the absence or high presence of this hormone at the fetus's developmental stage. For example, in some animals such as guinea pigs, adult males deprived of testosterone during fetal growth were less likely to mount other animals and more likely to allow other guinea pigs to mount them (even if they happened to be the other males). In other words, the temperament to mount other animals or to permit being mounted upon in adulthood is determined by the high presence or low testosterone levels during early fetal brain development. In animal models, when newborn female rats are exposed to testosterone for a short period, as adults, they will more likely be attracted to female sex partners, and this is also true for male rats.[36] This has also been observed in pigs. Could this be also true in humans given our genetic resemblance to these animal species? Male homosexuality has also been observed in other species such as dragonflies, gut worms, barn owls, lions, and zebra finches (a type of fish).[37]

Another scientific explanation for queerness worth exploring is the genetic basis or better put, the interplay of genetic variation that may influence these genes' expression in behaviour. It is a known fact that not all genes are expressed, and different factors such as the social and physical environment have roles to play in how a gene is expressed. One specific aspect that comes to mind is stress. Some studies have shown that in one such research carried out on rodents that had a genetic mutation that did not allow both sexes of the rodents to convert testosterone to estradiol (a primarily female hormone).[38] In this case, the genetic mutation had already occurred, and the specific gene in question is the Cyp 19 gene. With the mutation of this gene already carried out, females tended to mount other rodents while males were willing to be mounted, which is counter-intuitive if you think about it. But that is how a gene can modulate behaviour. When the researchers injected the females with estradiol to counter testosterone production, females became more willing to be mounted by males.

Can you imagine what this proves? I found this study quite exciting, and I implore you to look for similar studies and perform your own unbiased quest into this topic of queerness for yourself to form your judgement. You may be surprised by what you discover just as I was. Science is interesting.

Bringing this long story home down to humans and in particular, children. These experiments that have been carried out in animal models would be impossible to undertake in humans today in the 21st century with all the ethical concerns involved. But that does not mean that the role of genes and hormones do not apply in humans. Beyond applying the same reasoning from animals to humans and making a guarded extrapolation, one genetic condition in human fetuses provides the perfect opportunity to test if what is observed in animals is true in humans. It turns out that it is also true in humans as I would like to now explain.

The human genetic disease is congenital adrenal hyperplasia or CAH. Although the condition can be corrected at birth, during fetal development, for CAH to arise, a genetic mutation has to occur that removes an enzyme responsible for the production of hormones in the adrenal gland, resulting in the over secretion of testosterone-like hormones. In males, this might not pose a problem since male fetuses are usually flooded with testosterone during development.

But what about females? Besides anatomical changes to their genitals, girls exposed having CAH usually engage in masculine rough play (although this sounds cliché), they are less likely to be interested in performing motherly roles with dolls as most female toddlers do and are generally more likely to prefer playmates with similar interests. In one systematic review published in 2020 of the available evidence (systematic reviews top the pyramid of evidence), some researchers showed that compared to the general population, females with CAH at birth had a stronger likelihood not to have exclusively heterosexual relationships while for males with the same condition at birth did not show the same tendency for mainly non-heterosexual relationships.[39]

It is worth reiterating that sexual orientation is mostly not a choice but a biologically set behaviour based on sexual affinity or attraction. I believe that this is not a choice because if it were, people should be free to move freely on the sexuality spectrum without any inhibitions. But how many of your friends or family have you witnessed becoming straight or gay overnight. If you have made any such observation, you probably got your friend or family member's memo late enough.

And as a continent, we Africans need to embrace the reality before us and shun all forms of antipathy towards queers. I think that most of the antipathy and physical and verbal violence meted to people who identify as gay in Africa result from fear of the unknown. If you take anything from this chapter, I would like you to conduct research yourself and find the truth that awaits you. A sense of peace and calm will overwhelm you as you come to realise like the scientist and two-time Nobel Prize winner, Marie Curie said, that, "Nothing is to be feared, it is only to be understood. Now is the time to understand more, so that we may fear less."

We must be honest enough to have open conversations with children about sexuality before they attain sexual maturity and discover for themselves, most times in a negative way, what end of the sexuality spectrum they are predisposed to. There is no need to bury our heads in the dunes of sand like ostriches and tell ourselves that children will either conform to society's trending expectations of them or that they will turn out as we think in our mind.

Whatever we tell them will do little to change their minds about their sexual orientation, but it will open the door of conversation and the path to liberation that makes them feel accepted and in every way part of their communities. We should be able to have such discussions from an unbiased point of view that can only be obtained by studying the facts of the matter rather than leaning on the crutches of religion or culture or being blinded by our whim's fantasies for our children's future.

Homophobia is a learned habit as no child is born homophobic. The church's culture stemming from its teachings on homosexuality serves to ingrain this thought pattern into the minds of children who would later become homophobic adults. This Church culture which spans beyond the Roman Catholic Church includes ostracism from the family, communion, and immediate society.

Think for a moment of the alternate portrayal of the Trinity by Hans Urs von Balthasar, where the Father is depicted fertilising the Son.[40] The consequences of such portrayal would have had a different effect in the world today. To state it plainly, church culture and indeed the catholic church is homophobic in its origins. Many centuries ago in the Middle Ages, the Catholic Church spearheaded a headhunt for gay individuals and encouraged its laity to hand them over to secular authorities for punishment (in many countries, the practice held a death penalty).

With the Spanish Inquisition's commencement, nearly a thousand individuals were tied and burned at the stake for practising sodomy.[41] In Nigeria, after President Goodluck Jonathan banned homosexual practices in the country, he garnered support for the Policy from Nigeria's Catholic and

Anglican spiritual leaders and from their adepts with Bishops writing him congratulatory messages for the heavy-handed law.

In our age, Pope Francis has openly discouraged gays from joining the catholic priesthood, it goes without saying that many men under the shadow of the Vatican's holy call to the priesthood are themselves secretly practising homosexualism. This is not new. One thousand years ago, the Catholic Church paid little attention to the homosexual practices within its clergymen.

Today, many priests complain of the suffocating feeling of being gay and at the same time being under the service of the church. What changed? In the Lateran church council held as far back as 1179 and chaired by Pope Alexander III, homosexuality was banned with the consequences for priests practising it ranging from being defrocked to severe penance and ex-communication. I believe that this subtle labelling of homosexuality as a grave sin has seriously contributed to the growth of homophobia across the world since most people on the planet listen to the church and do not want to miss the promise of eternal life in heaven.

In 2021, while the Catholic Church teaches in its catechism that having thoughts of same-sex relationship is innocuous but acting on those whims is not, for priests, it seems that they are held to a different standard.

Many priests who are gay fear for the consequences of their nature and they are often forced to remain in same-sex orders or monasteries and be personally responsible for anything that may send sparks to tinder and ignite a scandal. According to French journalist and author, Frédéric Martel who spent four years researching his book and conducting over 1,500 interviews with cardinals, bishops, monsignors, papal ambassadors, and Swiss guards, priests, and seminarians, 80% of the priests at the Vatican are gay.[42] Take a moment to think of what this means. Imagine how many priests you know who might actually be practising closet homosexuality while they put up a holy face raising the wafer at mass every day.

Would the catholic church one day, maybe centuries later apologise to humanity as penance for their role in homophobia like they did several aeons down the line for burning Giordano Bruno at the stake in the 1600s and imprisoning Galileo for their 'intellectual crimes' of disproving the geocentric theories the Holy see was promulgating and finally grant full recognition of the fact that some people are just born and mingle differently from the rest of us? Would Islam and Judaism do the same too? Wouldn't it make the world a beautiful place to be in?

From my tone, you would think that I have always been a saint and anything but homophobic as far as this topic is concerned. But I did not escape easily from the society I was raised in, at least not before it left a sad searing smear on my heart. Even I was not spared from the firm gridlock of homophobia in my formative years. As a child, I was sent off to an all-boys Catholic boarding school by my parents where I spent six years as a pre-teen and teenager under the military-like order of authority which existed between students in different levels of studies.

Often, students in higher classes (grades) would bully younger students and force them to perform some punishments in the form of drills or floggings. That makes me think of what a young military recruit in Westpoint goes through. Without saying much, students went through a lot of physical abuses besides having to cope with academic demands. This bullying was overlooked by the staff in charge of the students' welfare and was subtly encouraged.

When I was in my first year, a senior student in his final year of studies was caught and accused of having same-sex relationship with a younger student. His classmates who were the only ones who could exercise authority over him put him through physical torture by making him roll in the dirt while they poured water on his body and flogged him mercilessly with freshly cut canes.

He was made to walk naked around the school, this was to disgrace and humiliate him while many called him awful names. I must clarify that this was all carried out by pupils who were not older than 18 years. The question that begs for answer is; where did these young lads learn to be so homophobic and not mind their business. The least they could have done was report the case to the school staff for appropriate action to be taken instead of practising wild jungle justice on their own.

When I reached the apex of authority in that high school and had pupils in five classes below me who feared my jurisdiction and that of my classmates, a similar event repeated itself. This time, it came to the widespread knowledge that several students in junior grades had same-sex affections for younger students or their own classmates. Guess what we did as the new dictators of the school? We put them through the same gruelling torture. I can still remember the heavy burden of hate I bore and poured from my mind as I lashed them severally with fresh canes and made them serve severe physical punishments such as planting their head upside down on the bare floor without supporting the rest of their bodies with their hands. Their heads and feet were their only contact with the floor.

This particular punishment is hard, and I cannot even perform it without much stress to my body. But at the time, I didn't seem to have a problem with meting it out to these guys while thinking I was doing the right thing by possibly making them have a change of mind of these thoughts they were entertaining and acting upon. Unfortunately, my experience only leaves me to question if it has also somehow contributed to homophobia in society through how we were formed.

Today, among the Alumni of my high school, you can find many top-ranking military and civilian administrators who make vital decisions implemented in the Nigerian society. How far has that seed of homophobia which was allowed to flourish in our formative years gone today? Nowadays, often, I am full of regret when I think about these things, but I am thankful for the new thoughts that I have embraced now because it is worrisome to think what I would have become had I allowed society to dictate my thoughts and wield an influence on how I perceive other humans on this planet.

This kind of homophobia is epidemic in catholic schools around the world, such as in places as far as Australia and Canada and across the Eurasian continent's expanse. For example, in a qualitative study published in the journal of catholic education, a teacher in Queensland who participated in a survey recounted how a student died by suicide because he had difficulty negotiating to be gay in a Catholic microcosm, revealing critical knowledge about the little known phenomenon of religiously sanctioned homophobia existing in Catholic schools I have tried to elucidate in this chapter.

[43]The Catholic Church's position on sexual diversity is usually promoted in Catholic schools primarily through a curriculum taught through the mesh of a Catholic filter which silently breeds the culture of homophobic bullying. Many students have lost their lives to suicides or have put themselves in harm's way because of such policies.

It is difficult to agree on what age children could be said to attain the age of consent. Many nations around the world have varying age points when a child is said to have attained the age of consent. In Europe, it varies from as low as 14 to 18 years. What we are sure of is that their early teenage years herald the beginning of puberty. The age of puberty is a challenging time for parents who seem to always be at loggerhead with their teenage children who talk rudely to everyone in their crosshairs, some of them could be rebellious at this age, they wouldn't want to have a bath, some even decide to dye their hair violet, and the behaviour of others might be considered typically unsocial depending on the environment, some parents are often ignorant of the inner battlefield that torments their kids.

Beyond the biological changes in their bodies, teenagers usually begin to assert their sexual preference, which could go in a myriad of ways. Several factors determine this, such as genetic predisposition or simply put, epigenetics, a combination of how several biological changes might change DNA without necessarily changing its base sequence. Under the illusion of free will and within the confines of genetic and epigenetic influences, many will be attracted to the opposite sex. Because nature always has a way of balancing things out, in any case, however, there will, as a matter of fact, be many others who would be attracted to the same sex. Are they any less human for having same-sex attractions or are their natural sexual instincts under the providence of their biological makeup not valid? These are questions parents must ask themselves in the 21st century, especially in societies where sexual freedom is repressed, particularly in many African countries and the Middle East.

But the story thankfully is not all grim in Africa. In June 2019, Botswana rescinded its anti-gay laws paving the way for progress in Africa. In a landmark ruling, Judge Michael Leburu declared that "the anti-sodomy laws are a British import developed without the consultation of local peoples." Four countries in Africa hold the death penalty for homosexuality with more than half of the countries having anti-gay laws.

These homophobic laws seem to be relics of the British colonial era, and there is a correlation of former colonies in the commonwealth of which Nigeria and Uganda are members. As stated earlier in this chapter, before the European colonisation of Africa, people were quite tolerant of gays. For example, dating back to 2400 BC excavated tombs has revealed two men embracing what has been interpreted as a show of intimate affection.[44] Centuries ago, most African countries had no binary interpretation of gender like the Europeans. I challenge you to name an African country that showed persecution of gays for their orientation before colonisation. For example, the Yoruba and Igbo tribes in present-day Nigeria did not have a binary gender world view for their new-borns and even today, many African languages do not have a binary assignment of terms. And in the ancient kingdom of Sudan, female children of monarch descent were often given slave girls for their sexual pleasure. The arrival of the British, with their Christian values, changed the face of this all-inclusive African culture on sexuality.

In gradual but sure steps and in several African countries, despite many cruel laws against them, gay citizens and their allies are spearheading the movement to ensure that such laws are repealed. A safe environment can be created for anyone to grow up into the sexuality they are hardwired to or choose for themselves rather than waiting for a saviour from faraway lands to come and rescue them. I really hope that the African continent gets it right. Following the resounding success in Botswana, I hope that this will open the discussion on what being gay or transgender means across the continent on the different sexual identities that one may be born into, decide to take up or feel drawn to, over a warm fire in many families starting from Botswana across the remaining vast expanse of the birthplace of humanity-Africa.

CHAPTER

8

ARTIFICIAL INTELLIGENCE, TRANSHUMANISM AND CHILDREN

"What is a human being, then? 'A seed.' 'A ... seed?' 'An acorn that is unafraid to destroy itself in growing into a tree."
- David Zindell

In Africa, and most parts of the world, things seem to still be done traditionally as they were done seventy years ago despite the ubiquitous computing and the rise of modern technology. Most people are raising the children of today in the exact way they would have raised them almost seventy years ago. The shocking reality is that while we have certain cultures suited for the industrial economy, we are presently living in a very prosperous information or computer age that we haven't really learned to master fully just yet. The exciting thing about this Information Age is the speed with which things develop. The Industrial Revolution started over 300 years ago and ended just about less than 40 years ago, crossing into the Information Age. Compared to the end of the Agricultural revolution, although the Industrial revolution picked up quite fast since the invention of tools like the wheel and the steam engine, we have now made much more progress in the Information Age than the time between the Agriculturally based economy to the Industrial economy. In our world today, new technology is released annually, and it is becoming increasingly challenging to keep up with the frontiers that are being traversed in information technology.

The ongoing technological revolution in the world is a good thing. If you take the time to appreciate what devices, data and connectivity are at your disposal from the standpoint of a human alive just over a century ago, your mind would be blown away with awestruck wonder. There is no doubt about the stewardship that rests on our shoulders as we direct science and technology. Humans are seriously on the way to colonising mars already with the significant advancements being made by private individuals and governments. With the considerable breakthroughs in this plan to get the human species to become an interplanetary species, our recent successful hitchhiking of a probe on a comet would seem like child's play-and a far cry from what we are capable of accomplishing tomorrow. The reductionism of nanotechnology has blessed humanity with lifesaving stents inserted into a blood vessel and whole fabricated immune cells which are artificial to provide support, prevent and fight diseases. With the digitisation of most analogue procedures, I still cannot say if all these are for better or worse, although I am enjoying the development of things immensely. Such a question would be better answered by someone else who has lived through the doorway of both eras.

One problem we could face might be the underutilisation of these technologies due to the machine-gun-rate they are being churned out at us. As a result, we have so much more software to solve a single problem while other problems sit unattended to for years. It is like the coal mining days again. Once coal was discovered in a specific place, everyone went there with their diggers and shovels ready to disembowel the earth. It is the same phenomenon we face today. When a particular problem is targeted by software developers, all other software developers cannot think of any other problem that needs to be solved. We have gotten to a point where we have the same development issues on the lips of everyone and the same method of tackling it to tag along-be it poverty, migration, healthcare delivery, or the displacement of persons; when we think about the problem, everyone has their software ready for that single problem that might not even have a significant impact if it is solved. It is as if the technological race we are all involved in today is designed to impress one another rather than resolve problems. If this is the case, then we must reform our thinking and address one problem at a time with one tool at a time from our box of technological solutions rather than doing otherwise.

The experts at the producing end of these most engaging technologies we have seen yet must cross-pollinate their ideas while at the same time maintaining their individuality in problem-solving to avoid repetitive innovations. If they successfully implement this, we will have societies with an infinite armamentarium of solutions for problems as they arise. We would genuinely then reap the fruits of the 21st century and although I agree with scientist and philosopher, Rene Dubos when he said, "Natural and cultural forces will overcome technological and political imperatives and continue to nurture the genius loci which accounts for the persistence of place", I am convinced that even him would have his jaws drop if he could see now, how fast, and proficiently we are going in our time.

Children particularly can be made or marred by these astronomical technological developments. This is not a speculation of something that might happen in the future, but it is actually happening now, and with each passing day, the impact of fast-moving technology such as Artificial Intelligence continues to reshape the face of the world children occupy.

Perhaps one way these fundamental shifts in societal dynamics between machines and humans can be explained, taking into account tomorrow's children's implications is through the abstract strategic board game of Go. With experts dating the first Go game to around 2, 500 years ago in ancient China, it has beaten other board games like chess and checkers as one of the oldest board games played by humans. The creation of the game has been mainly attributed to Emperor Yao of ancient China who invented it to teach wisdom to his stubborn son who would not read any book his parents offered him but only cared about combat. Go continues to be played around the world, even in post-modern times. The standard Go board is made up of 19 horizontal lines and 19 vertical lines crossing each other. It is played with black and white button-like placeholders called stones. Once a player places a stone on one of the line's vacant intersections, it can no longer be moved by the player.

When the stone is surrounded by an opponent's stones on all sides, the stone is then captured. The game was probably popularised by the aristocrats in ancient China since it was studied as one of the four necessary arts of their class which also included playing a stringed instrument (the guqin), calligraphy and painting.

With the possibility of as many combinations of strategy as the human mind can conceive, no two Go games played at any point in human history are the same, and it is said that Go is even spiritual because each game is a creation that would never be repeated due to the way the game's strategic sequences differ from each other. To be a master Go player of even modest repute requires that you tap deeply into the bottomless wells of human creativity and ingenuity.

As a 9th dan Go player, South Korean master Lee Se-dol ranks as one of the best players of this ancient game in modern times and has won several international championships making him one of the most formidable in this area in modern times. However, recently, Lee was usurped by an Artificial Intelligence computer program leading to his retirement from playing Go publicly.

[45] Named AlphaGo, this AI has lived up to its nomenclature by becoming the Alpha organism in the game of Go and demonstrates what AI is capable of accomplishing in our world. Played in 2016, against AlphaGo in Seoul, for a $1 million prize, the five-game match between human and machine was widely broadcast to both Go aficionados and computer science lovers across the world.

No one could at the beginning of the game predict in what way the match would go. Would it be a win for the inanimate, but seemingly conscious AI-AlphaGo invented by Google Deep mind who have a goal to develop artificial intelligence or will humans who have been the Alpha species for as long as history has documented win once again like they have done in all areas of physical existence? To be fair to the Go master, even if he first assumed that he was going to win all 5 games in the match which took place on five different days, he was only able to win one game after losing others to resignation or outright losses making AlphaGo a world champion in this ancient game that showcases the wonders of human creativity. This marked a change in AI and spelt a future where AI might come to dominate the centre space of human activity. This was not news though because experts in computing had always predicted that a day like this would come and writers of science fiction such as Isaac Asimov had given away glimpses of such novel technology-dominated future. As I write these words, many advancements in AI are being made at mind-boggling speed every day. No one knows what the future would look like let alone how children of the world are supposed to navigate it. Yet it is for these children that we struggle to sign peace accords, develop agriculture and other sustainable technologies that have the potential to make tomorrow much better than today.

Artificial Intelligence is gradually tearing apart the cultural curtains which have for centuries separated humanity in the form of language barriers. With AI, it is becoming increasingly easier to learn new languages and communicate across societies even if we don't speak the language organically. It will soon be possible for a child born today to communicate across cultures seamlessly in the dawn of such a young life. Natural language processing, which is a blooming field mixing linguistics, artificial intelligence, and computer science to understand the interactions between natural human language and a computer's way of processing them, has revolutionised how we communicate compared to just less than twenty years ago. Every time I travel to a new country where I cannot speak the language, I employ my phone's translator connected to the internet, to help me read signs, tickets, and order in restaurants. Perhaps the most interesting was when I spoke French to my young nephew in London, and he asked me to spell out the words so that he could translate them on his mum's phone. He is certainly not the only child who performs this modern magic. Millions of children employ artificial intelligence services to figure out the nuances of foreign languages through natural language processing.

Entrepreneurs have developed question answering robots through natural language processing to meet the needs of children worldwide and make their childhood more technologically advanced. While I perceived the sophisticated technology of my childhood through cartoons and computer games, children today with a high machine quotient (how children easily familiarises themselves to a machine's operation), can interact with the characters in the books they read and the cartoons they watch, this is made possible by the wonders of AI. This makes learning very dynamic for a child born in the 21st century. One can only imagine how this kind of technology is being deployed to help with early childhood education through chatbots and smart toys in the more developed corners of the world, like in Japan.

Put together, it seems that the fusion of the science of AI technology and the arts has happened. This will play a large role in language acquisition, and the development of different types of cognitive skills in the right and left-brain hemisphere of children born in this age of information revolution. While a polyglot of the far past like Sir Richard Burton may have been able to speak more than a dozen languages in decades and even sneak himself into the holiest Islamic city, Medina, by speaking fluent Arabic even before the rise of modern technology, more modern teenage hyperpolyglots like Timothy Doner have been able to master as much as a quarter of a hundred in less than half a decade at just seventeen years old using technology.[46] Artificial Intelligence has the potential to enable children to break even more barriers than that. It is only a matter of time, and AI keeps getting better at understanding humans and how we learn even as it remains a bit esoteric to most humans.

Based on the personal data which we all generate by using the internet and the rise of the Internet of things (IoT), children could have personalised AI tutors who understand them deep down to their most personal idiosyncrasy and could accompany them throughout life providing teaching customised to strengthen their weaknesses and build upon their strengths. It seems that the educational opportunities of the children of the next generations would be better than the best education which is available to wealthy families today. The deployment of smart software and other information technology tools already during the coronavirus pandemic lockdowns in different countries highlight this.

I have heard from some children that they really enjoy online learning and the use of their personal communication tools, although they complain about the absence of their friends' physical presence. In Africa, in addition to the lack of physical problems, my interaction with some children revealed that the best deployment of "software" which they got in their schools was the use of WhatsApp to send assignments to their teachers and receive long notes. I personally cannot imagine how inconvenient this would be, but they seemed to not mind. This is the beginning of the digital divide of inequality that technology can bring if we do not act early to reverse this trend.

While the impact of the information revolution in simplifying human activities like communication between people located in two different continents, or the calculations and analyses performed for us by software, it is not exactly easy to measure or at least judge how useful the information revolution has been on the cognitive abilities of adults exposed to nascent information technology tools in their childhood. Doing that would mean that we can say without an iota of doubt that everything about the information revolution challenges the human mind to perform at a higher plane of existence. Neuroscientists and computer scientists usually collaborate to evaluate behavioural and digital data to observe and measure digital stimulation's impact on cognitive development in children. According to some Italian scientists, children with superior digital skills seem to have better cognitive development in areas like language semantics and with significant improvements in logical reasoning and visual memory.[47] Children who enjoy digital stimulation related to pleasure early in life from tools such as video games and computers seem to show a favourable steady increase of cognitive skills and perhaps intellectual capacity in a world connected to the information highway and "digital universe".

This means that there would be disparities or inequality created through the uneven access to these information technology tools described above by children of the world, especially in sub-Saharan Africa. This could mean that while the rest of the world prepares for the next shift in the Information Age, children in these emerging countries are being prepared for the Industrial Era which has faded away from this century's reality. Whatever relics of the Industrial Era that remains in our world today is only akin to the muscular dance performed by a serpent whose head has been crushed.

A lot remains to be done to close the digital divide that separates the global north from the worldwide south in terms of literacy and the development of cognitive skills necessary to navigate a digitalised world. To not repeat past mistakes, developers of AI should create their programs with the same biases that foster inequality through the digital divide in their minds. Considering that children in Africa are already on the wrong side of this divide, it is necessary that any future developments in AI and information technology, no matter how futuristic and fast-paced takes into consideration areas like children education and life skill development in a way that does not further alienate unfortunate children from the classrooms-whether they are digital or brick-and-mortar classrooms. Instead, it would be advantageous to focus on making these AI technologies more accessible and ubiquitous even in tough to reach corners of the world so that exponential knowledge can be within reach of every child on the planet. Doing this would ensure that the world is genuinely prosperous and that children are prepared for a digital future that awaits them through a glass membrane.

As we prepare children for a digital future, we must all be aware of the threats to the status quo fostered by the Information Age revolution with AI technology as its taskmaster. Almost every field of human endeavour and professional quest will be affected in due time by these technological cataclysms. Some domains which have already taken the first significant hits include the healthcare, finance, legal, transport and logistics industries. More specific fields will join this list as the decades of the second millennium roll by. I would like to briefly discuss the healthcare and legal industries as prime examples. Although it might be challenging to replace doctors, however, this doesn't mean we should tell children not to dream and aspire to becoming one, the way a medical diagnosis is performed for certain pathologies is a significant leap from the time of Hippocrates in ancient Greece which only makes me wonder if we are at the cusp or peak of these developments in medicine. For example, while it was formerly a matter of probability contingent on a surgeon's skills, precision surgeries are already taking place with the help of AI-powered robotic surgeons that reduce the margin of error in surgical procedures to almost zero, thereby increasing the chances of survival even for the most dangerous medical complications due to human errors.

The beauty of AI is that it can learn from processes like machine learning and deep neural networks to improve each time as opposed to humans who can only learn from their experiences and have a cap on how much information they can process at a time. A much-anticipated project in AI-assisted robotic surgery is a project called "Optimus" in Spain which aims to take advantage of the rollout of 5G technology to enable surgeons to perform surgery using robots, AI and telecommunications at a reduced latency rate (response time of the surgical devices) without being physically present in the operating theatre.[48] Using deep neural networks which are AI systems that imitate organic (human) intelligence to diagnose medical conditions like cancer and some infections is already the order of the day in many parts of the world. The system is perfected every day as the AI systems gather more data to improve their ability to perform an accurate diagnosis of, say cancer. Artificially intelligent radiological systems are as good as human radiologists in diagnosing cancer if not better. While a human radiologist has trained qualitatively with a minimal number of radiological images starting from medical school, through deep neural networking, AI technology can learn and perfect the rudiments of radiology with high reliability via training with databases containing millions of patient scans collected by regional health systems.

Even with its reputation of being very conservative and packed with Luddites, according to experts, the legal profession is one of the sectors of the human sphere that undergo major upheavals due to the revolution of the Information Age with AI technology and computer science at its forefront. Children who dream of becoming lawyers and judges would have to make adjustments to their game plan as the 21st century unfolds before our eyes, stunning us each day with innovative technology that courageously replaces the old modus operandi. The legal industry is worth more than one trillion dollars globally. Its influences like an octopus's arms span almost every kind of business that has been conceived by humans from agriculture, art, education, science and engineering and computer sciences itself.

Every contract needed to ensure the smooth sail of a venture usually requires the blessing of at least a lawyer or a body with the necessary legal jurisprudence over the parties involved. Because both law and machine learning which is a crucial aspect of artificial intelligence both use similar systems in their operation in that they both refer to history to predict how they should behave in the present and use both the past and the present to stipulate actions for the future, this makes the legal profession particularly vulnerable to automation using artificial intelligence since the structured thought process is already established in the former.

For instance, while it is comparatively easier to initiate most contracts legally, monitoring changes in the agreements between parties can be difficult for a human to achieve with accuracy albeit necessary. Artificial Intelligence through neural networks offers the hope that this could be delegated to a machine, resulting in more free time for lawyers or completely replacing their services. How then should children who dream of adjudication in their adult lives work towards their objective? Should they completely abandon this noble profession? The automation in the legal profession would result in cheaper, faster, and more efficient legal systems, especially for many countries where finding a lawyer and getting the jury's judgement can take ages. It is not that Artificial Intelligence will replace the jury, that would be a difficult argument to make, but it could simplify the demands of members of a jury.

Building an argument to save a client's money or neck in a lawsuit is also getting faster through litigation prediction using artificial intelligence where the intelligence machine comes up with different scenarios even before the real showdown in a courtroom. One of the first areas in the legal profession to certainly give in to Artificial intelligence is the research that needs to be carried out by legal experts on cases daily. Already, there are smart networks which lawyers can join that helps this kind of research to be completed in a matter of minutes as opposed to poring through hard copies of every case file in their country.

For children, this means that in conjunction with learning the hard skills required for most traditional professions, they will now have to be capable of interacting with and managing intelligent systems made possible by silicon chips. There is now an excellent reason for children to be educated to take advantage of these new job possibilities even as old ways of doing things go extinct or obsolete through automation. This is the time to look at automation as an ally rather than as the devil because it also holds the potential to create new job opportunities.

According to former COO of Microsoft, Kevin Turner, "The only job security we have is our individual commitment to personal development." That seems to be something good enough that teachers of children preparing them for their adult lives in a fast-paced world could start with. I would add that building creativity and interdependency would also be highly necessary for such a world. Jobs which will be safe from the AI revolution would certainly require creativity and would most likely be jobs in which the working environment is unpredictable and in which humans can apply the biological problem-solving skills to seek solutions even while they collaborate across different fields.

Not every one of us gives a warm reception to the idea of raising children for an AI dominated world. Cultural barriers exist in the proliferation of AI. I recollect an incident that occurred to me and a few of my friends I ran into at the airport in Nigeria, several years ago while on a solo trip to Abuja Nigeria. It was 3pm, and we were already checked-in and boarded ready for taxiing and take-off. While seated, I caught up with a lovely lady who sat beside me, with a great smile and warmness, we took the conversation to a new level, I could remember it was on the recent gains made on automation, biotechnology, and nanotechnology that we were off to when suddenly, we heard someone scream out loud with a bang on the floor as if someone or something fell to the ground.

There was total silence now, the voice continued emphatically, a strain of sound effects and sounds to it, a monotone which accompanies fear and apprehension, as she screamed for help and called on the inflight hostess who soon appeared as a first responder to the scene, we were seated at mid-row seat 14 A, B, C, and she sat around 17D, E, F, or something like that. I could see to an extent what was happening, those not seated in a frantic manner all settled into their seats and the row was made free and cleared for easy access and movements within the cabin room, the captain had no other choice but to momentarily suspend the flight take -off operation. At the same time, we waited for the paramedics to arrive and evacuate her to the hospital.

While we waited for help, she was claustrophobic with an extensive or increased amount of apprehension that was believed to have amplified her state, causing her to perspire and gasp for breath instantaneously. As with all humans just as we could tell, the nature of the story kept everyone seated on the edge of our seats, even while we continued with the journey eventually a few more minutes later, presumably 15 minutes, no one found the courage to raise the topic.

We all felt good that we could eventually continue on the trip, most folks who had interviews or confirmed appointments on that flight held steady, but there was a lesson to be learnt as we would find out later.

Unbeknownst to us, she was a career medical professional from an elitist hospital in Abuja, she had been diagnosed of this condition some years earlier but she had suffered from it for over 10years until the diagnosis, she was initially a career educationist with an ivy degree working in a respected and reputable institution of higher learning until her condition led her into the field of medicine, her personal life and career led her to inspire the courage to make herself better, irrespective of the fewer opportunities within the country as at that time to find help, a fellow passenger who knew her told the story to us with this unique sense of courage and we finally felt a relief when the captain called out our attention just as we taxied to disembark that the inflight patient who was medically evacuated just before take-off was yet alright and was billed to get attention at a privately owned hospital in Cyprus at the behest of a concerned fellow passenger who witnessed what had happened.

We called it a day, but the lessons of that day and the critical nature of that condition helped me. The lovely lady who sat beside me on that flight with whom I initiated a conversation which centred around the medical world and the challenges we face as everyday Nigerians, the reality that she was appointed to get medical attention or help oversee overshadowed the situation that was happening all around us, we have since become good friends in the real sense of friendship, she now lives in Cyprus with her son as a single mother working as a field analyst for a French company into real estate and logistical services, her name is Ngozi Ada.

Though we discussed automation and the future of Artificial Intelligence on the plane, she seemed to be a Luddite and pessimistic about the rise of these smart machines. When we first spoke, she imagined that computers were taking people's jobs and it would only be a matter of time before robots would be appointed to help the woman who was suffering from claustrophobia taking out the human touch from life. In Cyprus, however, she works fluidly with advanced forms of these AI algorithms and machine learning at the logistics company she works with. Now, we laugh at it all whenever I call her. Children should also be nudged towards bravery instead of fear in the face of the revolution of the Information Age.

This new reality illustrates the story of how we as humans would have to continue to evolve and dig deeper into areas of human consciousness which were considered unthinkable in the past.

Many of the humans alive today can associate these changes with the dotcom era. There is a lot this new generation of humans can relate to, especially in the field of medicine, finance, and meteorology, for instance. The above experience illustrates the importance of the quality of thoughts we should build into the minds of the next generation. How we have come to this fantastic pinnacle of our collective grace remains a wonder, but for now, we need to conclude that the many things which we haven't accomplished yet as species lie in the fact that we are held back by our mental state of reasoning like Ngozi was. I am sure that for us to prepare children for their future and fully reap the benefits of this new age, we will have to embrace the one vital attribute of curiosity to overcome our self-imposed restrictions.

As a teenager growing up in Nigeria, the brim norm back then was that there were just about a few more strides for humanity to make before closing the curtains. In a way, this long-standing tradition held by the countless folks retained many promises for those who had fashioned their minds and mainly addressed their thoughts in line with this misconstrued assumption. While it lasted, I was also part of the generation who have suffered the negativity of this outcome, a position I have since worked my mindset to disavow.

What we failed to understand in this conversation is that the advantage or advantages of these recent breakthroughs in advanced technology and as a result of improved communication between our reasoning, and our understanding of the world we occupy has contributed more than enough new evidence that we have a lot more to benefit, despite what the many conservatives think. Mostly, the hesitation shown by many individuals in the world is due to fear of the unknown and apprehension to changes in the status quo.

The relationship between a new breakthrough and our origin is everything else along the line of observed things. In a group conversation, I have said to someone that my personal hint about what a new discovery does to its relationship with an older era technology, is much more than creative destruction. As we know it just like intelligence, the information does a few different things to our different mindsets, it belittles folks who are intimidated by it and gives a more splendid array of conformity in conscience to those who understand its importance, no matter if they are children or adults. But I am biased towards exposing children to progressive information because as the saying goes, "…the best time to plant a tree was 20 years ago." It will be sad for children born in the era of AI to feel uneasy while taking possession of their time.

In another isolated instance on a fixed offshore platform, a group of young men working for a drilling company were held spellbound by an intense conversation about their future. Men who were formerly young boys growing up in different parts of Nigeria, the exciting part of the discussion centred around the likelihood of them getting pushed out of jobs by the recent efforts at establishing alternatives to the insalubrious fossil fuels they work with. During the coffee break that followed, they all spoke with one voice, individual after individual they all spoke out in referential terms about how they felt about the potential possibility of biofuels, battery-powered automobiles fused with AI, smart aircraft, the inroads made into sustainable energy, the investment made by the International Oil Companies (IOC's) and the perceived body language of the western world towards its planned transition to crude oil alternatives.

This conversation lasted for a whole hour as the coffee break proved insufficient to the gathering for a whole lot of diverse reasons. Eventually, a senior citizen, a much more experienced and knowledgeable man amongst thcm, spoke out after hearing all their arguments. In his very brief contributions, it was made clear that if they all wanted a stake in the new world of renewable energy as it unfold; and if they all desire to partake in the new energy game evolving, then they all needed to brace up and expect the assurances of an evolving world as the new normal. He closed his statements by saying that stakeholders in the new world would have to do the needful. Their efforts should include technical considerations which will in coreferential terms include updates and upgrades to their skills and proficiency levels, acquiring the required skills to make themselves available to the market and an eventual goal of making themselves a part of the new world as not just stakeholders but policy drivers. This should be the same message that we should start to inculcate in children right from kindergarten even before they decide on what careers they want to pursue. The future is now.

Some countries of the world are blessed by what I would term a stroke of cultural luck that allows them to embrace the Information Age in its entirety. On the one hand, it has been observed that nations whose culture is mostly based on a Judeo-Christian narrative tend to fear hierarchy and are therefore usually afraid of AI-powered technology like smart robots. I believe this is one factor among many, responsible for the lagging behind in robotics and AI that we see when we visit these countries that did well in the Industrial Age. On the other hand, countries whose culture is based on philosophies directed at self-liberation as a form of spirituality, fare better in warmly embracing the advances of independently minded

AI or robotics technology due to their belief in the possibility of co-existence and equal responsibility sharing. For instance, in Japan, where the Shinto religion has been prevalent for thousands of years, even if it was only christened in 6th century AD to make a distinction between Buddhism and other religions present in old Japan. The Shinto religion has no founder and no central authority, no preaching or propaganda to spread it. But it is deeply ingrained in Japanese culture and defines the way people behave whether they are Shintoists or not.

Shintoists have as many as eight million divine spirits, gods or kami that are venerated within the Shinto intersubjective reality. Throughout the country, in monuments, shrines, and modern popular Japanese culture, references are made to them, and it has always been believed that they can possess inanimate objects. Joi Ito in his childhood like many Japanese children grew up watching anime like Neon Genesis Evangelion in which there is a lot of reference to an age in which man and machine are fused together to form more powerful and effective cybernetic organisms(cyborgs).[49] This inspires many kids right from childhood to look ahead for a future where they dream of becoming bionic cyborgs themselves. I have seen videos of restaurants in which robots take orders in Kyoto on the internet. Japan is undoubtedly one country I would love to visit myself to experience this creative space that humans have been able to build for themselves. It is as if they were born ready for the future, but this is not merely a stroke of luck, and something beyond the reach of countries in say, Africa. We can start now and upgrade how we introduce the world to children to be ready for this new age.

The West and countries influenced by them have a problem with every object possessing a spirit, but the Japanese do not. As a matter of fact, this is the order of the day, even in modern-day Japan. Sadly, this is similar to the animist culture that pervaded Africa before the arrival of Christianity and Islam. In Japan, therefore, it is not difficult for a young student to imagine that AI is the computer having a mind of its own and that it can be fused with a robot to perform even more human-like tasks. While these differences might be little, they go a long way in influencing how quickly people embrace and adapt to a world governed by information highways which seem to work more and more like the human mind. But whatever we choose to think on the matter, I believe that certain cultures are more prepared through no effort of theirs for the advances of this new era.

However, the honour of being the first human cyborg does not go to Japan despite their warm attitude to this kind of technology. The first-ever human-cyborg is a Spanish born British-Irish man called Neil Harbisson. I first heard of Harbisson from my friend in late 2014, and even though he has been a cyborg since 2004, the news didn't filter in early enough to me. However, my mind was not so open to the possibilities of the Information Age, and I somehow imagined that things would stale with word processors, email and maybe video calls. In 2004, I would have simply waved off the fact that an operation was done on him, and a cyborg antenna was attached to his head and emanating from his occipital bone as impossible-at least in function. But what did I know? Harbisson was born in 1984 with achromat vision-meaning that he was born colour blind. I think he was born at a good time as far as the rise of modern technology is concerned.

To correct his vision, Harbisson conceived and began designing the antenna in 2003 as a college student with the help of several experts.[50] While it was not easy to convince the ethics committee on the need or rationale for the surgery at the time, he was able to have the surgery performed secretly by unnamed doctors. With his antenna, he can hear and feel colours and communicate with satellites since the antenna is connected to the internet. Besides the usual colours, on the colour spectrum, he can also perceive ultraviolet and infrared which we can't see. To augment his perception of time and be in touch with Albert Einstein's theory of relativity, Harbisson has installed a solar crown which orbits his head slowly in 24 hours with a point of heat which he uses to judge the passage of time. He also communicates using morse code with a designated person through a bluetooth enabled tooth installed in his mouth. One of the craziest things is that his trusted friends can alter some aspects of his dreams from across the world by sending images and colours even while he sleeps.

He is a pioneer and a real man-machine fusion, and this has opened the door of possibilities for such technological marriages to be performed as time goes by. He is certainly not the last of the cyborg generation as people like Professor Kevin Warwick, Jens Naumann, Jesse Sullivan, Claudia Mitchell (the first female cyborg) and others continue to join this list of "superhumans." Children who know about this are beginning to get excited at this possibility for themselves too. No child wants to miss out on an opportunity to be a superhero.

Having accepted the possibility that humans can be fused to more intelligent systems integrated with AI or any of the fruits of the Information Age, I cannot hold myself back from asking some questions. Will children be able to choose for themselves if they want to be superhuman cyborgs? If society allows them to, what could be the implications of such a choice? Would the "human" rights arena undergo yet another revolution and revisit of the first principles and definitions of what it means to be a living being with rights? With the pace of advancements in this age, some questions that parents, communities, and governments would have to ponder both nationally and internationally.

Ray Kurzweil, inventor, futurist, and author, makes it more explicit in his book Singularity is near, foretelling that when humans start to upgrade their organs and features to more robust mechanical and intelligent systems, every parent might want their child to be smarter, more dexterous, or more handsome. This might create a sort of enhancement race and competition between families and ultimately between societies which may drive the division on the inequality scale further apart. Affluent families and countries would tend to have better-equipped children if we can judge a child's worth by how many beeping gizmos are running through her body.

When Chinese biophysicist, He Jianku announced the birth of twin girls some years ago, nothing would have seemed unusual about twins' birth since this occurrence happens every now and then. What aroused the interest of the press and the global community, however, was that he had, first of all, edited the genome of some embryos using a genetic engineering technology called CRISPR.[51] He then implanted the genetically edited embryos in a woman's womb which resulted in the birth of the twins. Like that, he had sneaked into an era of science where the human species' gene pool can be tinkered with and rewritten. He did this by damning the ethical consequences which stood in the way of his leaping act.

Perhaps the world was not ready for such a rude shock. Therefore, many tiny ethical cracks that existed in the minds of scientists and bioethicists became broad divisions. While most people condemned the act based on ethics and the assertion that humans should not tamper with our own genetics because we do not know what the results will be, others gladly rejoiced and welcomed a new era for humans, and I quite believe that those scientists were contacted by expectant mothers on the possibility of making a tweak here or there in their unborn child. The ensuing debates seemed to be divided into two camps, some thought that the bad publicity of gene editing was terrible for the field whether or not the goal was to make editing human genome a standard or common procedure while other bioethicists and scientists thought that the scandal could result in forward propulsion of gene editing. Gene editing has the potential to halt processes such as premature ageing in children-a currently incurable genetic disease called progeria. The life span of children with this disease is 15 years. To mention, another condition which could potentially be eliminated include the life-threatening sickle cell anaemia, which disproportionately affects people of African origin. An ethical question worth asking is, now that we have the tools to act, should we let nature run its course in these children's earthly sojourn with their lives lasting as long as a single ocean wave? Or should we intervene to extend their lives?

What will happen when artificial intelligence, cyborgs and gene editing become commonplace, and all we have to do is choose? This is a dilemma worth considering because it is only a matter of time before the seemingly impossible meets us at our doorsteps again as time unfolds. Will we be ready to respond?

Many believe we are already living through the transhuman era and think it may have been going on for longer than we cared to notice. But are children capable of conceiving transhuman desires even as they observe the world through their coloured lenses? Transhumanism is a philosophical movement and concept that aims to advocate for the use of available technology to enhance human physiology and intellect. People like Neil Harbisson who also doubles as an activist for cyborgs are transhuman and so are people who also desire such enhancements whether they have succeeded in acquiring it or not.

There are debates on the origin of the transhuman movement, but many can trace it to the German philosopher Friedrich Nietzsche who coined the term Übermensch, meaning "overhuman". While he thought that the time will come when humans will again be part of an evolutionary leap, Nietzsche believed that humans had a finite amount of will-to-power which he called quanta that according to him, existed in a form whose fundamental reality is preservation and enhancement of power. And these were acquired by an adult and could not be passed on to his descendants.[52] Children can become who they are by chance or through deliberate action, and this is a transhuman thought line. As it is often repeated in their circles, "The bible said that God made man in His own image. The German philosopher Ludwig Feuerbach said that man made God in his own image. The transhumanists say that humanity will make itself into God." [53] When you look at it, even a religion like Christianity can be said to be transhuman in the sense that most Christians look forward to an eternal life in a more enhanced corporeal reality. Since Christian thought has dominated most of the West and the countries they influence, one wonders why many bioethicists are against modern transhumanism. Most of the arguments put forward by these bioethicists are usually based on whether an enhancement is permitted or whether it is desired (human rights). It has been argued by proponents of the movement that this debate should instead be shifted towards the questions about life's meaning because that seems to be what it is really about.

As I believe we are already in the dawn of a transhumanism era too, parents, communities and nations would have to wrestle with these questions themselves. Children may themselves be interested in becoming transhuman cyborgs or some form of enhancement with AI, and it would be necessary to answer justly if preventing them from accessible enhancements is not a violation of the very human rights we are trying to protect. Children may be forced soon to deal with the moral question of becoming immortal, which you can already discuss with your child if you choose to.

Let us not forget that transhumanism simply aims at improving the human condition through science and technology in fields like neuroscience, neuropharmacology, nanotechnology, artificial intelligence, and the attainment of an interplanetary species status. Elon Musk, innovator, and billionaire is pushing the frontiers, and it has been announced that Neuralink, one of his companies that manufactures implantable brain-machine interfaces (BMIs) through neurotechnology will go ahead with implanting these chips in the nervous systems of humans to cure paralysis and other diseases. Neuralink had already successfully implanted a similar chip in pigs previously.

Whatever side of the divide you stand on in the matters discussed in this chapter, we can all agree that at this moment in our developmental history, we should strive to educate our young minds to be the Masters of Technology by building their capacity before we let them take the reins from us with which they will ride humanity into its future. Will this future be a beautiful one or a dystopian one? I think the answer lies in the training we give today's children and how we introduce the concepts of artificial intelligence and transhumanism to them- as tools for our collective prosperity or as methods for separatist superiority. Moreover, to accomplish this incredible feat, children will need space and time in a liveable environment.

CHAPTER

9

THE ENVIRONMENTAL CONUNDRUM

———

"We did not inherit the Earth from our ancestors; we borrowed it from our children"
- American Indian proverb

s a young child searching for the truth of all life, I spent time studying Judeo-Christian religions that were geographically within my reach. The pang of fear and disappointment I felt at the apocalyptic and chaotic end promised for the end of life on Earth and which heralds the world's judgment had always troubled my mind growing up. But beyond the widest confines of my mind, this feeling that no matter what I did, the world would end in chaos built in me an insouciant attitude to nature and the environment around me. I am sure many adults and young children raised similarly in Africa can identify with this feeling. There was simply no point to care.

Whenever I read such books, the beautiful sunrises and sunsets in Nigeria no longer appealed to my sense of aesthetics; worse still, my friends, family and I dumped refuse like almost every other religious Nigerian without minding the negative impact this would have on the environment. The notion that it was not our problem, and any such problems of cosmic proportions was God's problem to fix, and that the problems prevail due to the apocalyptic stories that I grew up hearing and reading about.

In 1995, a pastor gave a talk on how the world was destined to end in Armageddon at a charismatic Christian meeting where I was present with my mum. It was a terrifying experience for a child like me in his first decade of life without mincing words. How could all this beauty go up in flames just like that when I only just arrived on this mysteriously alluring planet?

Amid the terror that had engulfed me, something stayed with me. I asked myself what if we humans could do something about it? As a child, I was told not to bother doing anything about it because it was our common destiny in the universe. I could not bring myself to believe that assertion.

Today, I know that despite all the chaos that goes on in numerous parts of the world from human causes and completely natural processes; we all have the power to decide in what direction we want to steer our destiny as a species and as custodians of life on Earth. Although I had always known that we could do something about it, it was difficult to believe due to my ingrained indoctrination even if I had outgrown it. The firm conviction that we as humans could do something about the environment and bequeath a safe and fecund planet with all its flora and fauna and the beautiful people and animals that live in it to the children of the future made the scales fall off my eyes in another meeting.

This time in Berlin, in 2015 at the World Health Summit as I listened to two professors argue about whether it was worth abandoning our planet and focusing on terraforming Mars and settling the human race there. The difference between the two meetings was that this time, I was surrounded by scientists who spoke my language and who saw possibilities and were willing to act for positive change. I learned that we can all act to save the planet. I believe this is the gospel we should preach to every child out there today.

It is no longer news within close circles around the world that our little blue planet in this universe is warming up steadily due to human orchestrated activities and non-human factors. Today, many people discuss global warming or climate change or have had to explain some strange physical phenomenon away with the term "climate change". This goes when the weather gets too warm, or when the streams remain dry, or when their communities are flooded. Our planet is ill, to say the least. The cascade of the different events that make the Earth warm up beyond levels that have been usually observed by available data has been termed global warming.

Global warming affects us all in the biosphere. According to National Geographic,[54] global warming is the culmination of several observable events such as melting glaciers in Antarctica, rising sea levels, dying cloud forests and dwindling wildlife that are a result of human-induced warming through the release of heat-trapping gases (greenhouse gases) which are now higher than any time as observed through computer models in the last 800 000 years.

Climate change and global warming are not new shows on planet earth. From back in the Earth's history around 11,500 years ago after the end of the last ice age, the climate on this planet warmed suddenly. This period of human history and rising temperatures since the last ice age, typically called the Holocene period by earth scientists, introduced a major change in human history dynamics. From being hunter-gatherers, our ancestors began to domesticate plants and animals in what has led to modern agriculture, and the debut of civilisation.

[55] Early populations depended on hunting, fishing, and foraging for wild plants. The abundance of plants and animals for foraging and hunting or fishing was determined by climatic trends. It has been postulated that ancient human societies were probably extremely vulnerable to the irregular climate than modern societies. They mostly depended on weather-sensitive crops instead of modern-day agriculture where many crops are available all year round. Still, this does not immunise 21st-century humans from the horrors of global warming and climate change because history has a funny way of repeating itself in ways, we have not yet

fathomed.

The atmosphere plays a crucial role in ensuring that life is possible on planet earth. It does this by warming up the Earth's surface with what is termed the greenhouse effect by blocking harmful ultraviolet radiation. This is all contingent on the right balance of gases in the atmosphere which all have their cycles defined by a series of interrelated chemical reactions. Terrestrial life or to put it better, biological activity and geological processes have played crucial roles in adding or removing gases like oxygen, carbon dioxide, and nitrogen from the atmosphere. Any unusual shift in the balance of these gases could be the cinders that send sparks and ignite an uncontrollable flame that could consume all life on Earth.

Although not strictly due to human activities alone, side by side with global warming, our planet is also undergoing fundamental shifts in its nature; this is termed climate change. Scientists use the term climate change to describe complex shifts in weather patterns and in the Earth's climate which is often characterised by short term cooling in some regions of the planet, at least for a short while.

Any fundamental change in the set rhythms that life forms in the biosphere depends on their physiological needs is termed climate change, and it could range from rising temperatures, rising sea levels, extreme and unstable weather conditions to a host of other environmentally impactful patterns that could affect everyday life all over a long period. However, let us not make the mistake of thinking that climate change does not encompass global warming. Because it does.

However, these terms are often used interchangeably to describe what we feel about the changes occurring in our physical environment. I would love that, beyond being right about what terms we employ in the spoken language, if we could all act together to reduce human impact on the world's ecosystems, then the use of these terms whether appropriately or not does not matter. So do not worry if you do not feel like there is a difference between them for now. We will delve deeper into the matter. These two events are not the same but act like a lousy quarrel between two mafia gangs in a community of law-abiding citizens.

But this time, as opposed to waiting like sitting ducks for a stray bullet to hit us, we can actually attempt to salvage the situation and stabilise our planet in all environmentally significant areas. The burden of global warming and cataclysmic climate change is especially often borne by vulnerable members of the human community-women and children. In a very complicated way, children's health is threatened by these environmental changes, the food security of their families is endangered forcing them to migrate to safer environments where these needs can be met as they avoid possible conflicts that could stem from the struggle for the control of natural resources.

For children in parts of the world where climate change effects are already being experienced, they experience a series of physical and psychological health conditions related to changing weather patterns, a myriad of infections due to altered disease patterns linked to the immediate environment. Besides these, it has also been postulated by climatologists and paediatricians that children could also suffer from heat stress or lung diseases related to heat stress which might arise from rising average global temperatures.

It is noteworthy that all these health changes are subtle and observed only when epidemiological models are employed along with climate science data. Without mincing words, climate change is a significant public health threat to all current and future children of the human race. Resulting from human activity in the previous centuries to contemporary human activity; climate change, geometric increases in the human population, the way we produce energy and consume it, how we interact with our habitat is putting severe pressure on our only planet. These observable and catastrophic changes threaten life in the biosphere on which the health, well-being and future of all children depend. At this point, I think it is noteworthy to state that many scientists and activists have said on different platforms that children have a fundamental right to inherit a planet in which they can raise their offspring.

With all the information we have accumulated about these anomalies, failure to reverse these negative environmental changes is akin to a violation of their fundamental human rights. Because of their underdeveloped physiology and metabolism, as well as higher exposure to air, food and water and their unique risk-seeking behaviour, children younger than five years old are at an increased risk of the effects of climate change on their health with children in the world's impoverished countries being disproportionately affected.[56]

The human body is equipped with a superb but limited heat regulation system. In the face of a cataclysmic rise in average habitat temperatures, it cannot perform optimally, resulting in heat-related abnormalities that can result in fatalities or mental stress. In the last five years since 2016, many parts of the world have experienced a series of heatwaves where the elderly and children carried the burden with recorded deaths. Although research on the association between the state of ill-health, mortality and heat exhaustion in children is limited, if we go by the data that we have on how rising temperatures affect the elderly who have a similarly vulnerable physiology and metabolism, then we will come into a full realisation of the adverse effects of this environmental factor. But we do not have to wait until we start seeing children in impoverished countries in the morgues before we accept that we have to act from a place of responsibility and duty to the future custodians of the planet.

Another aspect of children's health disturbed by these phenomena is how air quality affects their health. Already, in developing regions of the world such as in Africa and Asia, many children live with undiagnosed asthma which could worsen as a result of the decline in air quality due to air pollution. I once watched a documentary of a group of volunteers in an African country set up air quality monitors on trees and strategic areas in a village due to the community's epidemic levels in the community among children. Wildfires or the seasonal harmattan bush burnings in parts of West Africa include the release of carbon monoxide, particulate matter, and other chemicals affecting the ozone layer. The smoke can usually spread across thousands of kilometres having far-reaching effects in villages and small towns and it endangers the lungs of many children by inducing asthma. Not even non-asthmatic children are spared from these inconveniences due to their premature physiology.

Although not all scientists agree beyond a reasonable doubt, the pattern shifting effects of the climate due to global warming and climate change can be a precursor to a change in the dynamics of several infectious diseases to which children are vulnerable. Emerging infectious diseases and diseases formerly put under the guard of modern medicine and public health make a more robust return only to endanger these young ones' lives and decimate their population, thus disinheriting them of their earthly franchise.

There is enough reason to believe that with the rising global temperatures, infections like diarrhoeal microbes increase significantly. In contrast, lower temperatures are observed to be associated with a low incidence of these cases.[57] Global warming on its own has several effects on infectious diseases like vector-borne diseases, food, and water-borne diseases. Vector-borne diseases such as dengue and malaria spread to a broader geographical expanse due to the widening of the vector's warm habitat and influence (mosquitoes) across the globe. Some scientists have predicted that global warming will lead to the growth in dengue viral infections and the expansion of dengue virus endemic areas.[58]

These particular infectious diseases disproportionately affect children who are physiologically more vulnerable. Over one million people die of malaria each year with a considerable part of the statistic being children under five years old. It will be regrettable that despite the efforts of the global community such as, the World Health Organisation, the Bill and Melinda Gates Foundation and all their partners who try to fully reduce or eliminate these diseases, our failure to act on climate change and global warming can have adverse effects on the lives of the vulnerable children of the world.

The risk of infection with Vibrio cholerae, which causes cholera, is greatly influenced by the climate. Vibrio is responsible for about 120 000 deaths annually with young children in endemic areas being the most touched. Like malaria and dengue, elevated temperatures play an essential role in the transmission of cholera. Since the door is not yet shut upon us, we can still walk all of humanity through it to a prosperous future where we truly have the elements of nature under control or at least to the extent that we do not find it as a threat and in a state of existence where we are not a threat to nature itself.

Agriculture employs about 2.5 billion people and is one aspect of human activity that climate change negatively impacts, thereby putting food security at risk and exposing populations to the probability of starvation or undernourishment, and even famine. Broadly speaking, climate change affects all four dimensions of food security: food availability, food accessibility, food utilisation and food systems stability according to the Food and Agriculture Organisation of the United Nations.

Together, these threaten the livelihoods of individuals living on the planet, and as children depend on their families for nourishment and their overall well-being, they are the group with higher risk in the human community from climate-induced threats to food security. Although humans have achieved a remarkable feat in food security since the agricultural and industrial revolutions, this new threat which we face is like nothing we have experienced before. An estimated 821 million people worldwide are currently undernourished, with about 151 million children under five being stunted. Others suffer from nutrient and mineral deficiencies such as iron. This is not to say that climate change is solely responsible for this tumultuous route that humanity is heading towards. Factors such as exponential population growth, low-income growth and the over-dependence on animal-sourced proteins all work in concert with climate change and global warming to jeopardise the food system and economic livelihoods of billions of us.

According to studies which were carried out where climate change was singled out from other competing factors, food production of crops like maize and wheat have been negatively affected in low-latitude regions of the world by climate change particularly in Africa which is already battling with an undernourishment problem in some of its countries.[59] Already, current knowledge on climate change and global warming has shown that increasing temperatures, irregular rainfall patterns and the increased likelihood of sudden floods are harshly impacting food security.

According to the Intergovernmental Panel on Climate

Change, food security will continually be affected by climate change increasingly with the prices of cereals expected to rise significantly by 2050.

Children need an optimal level of nutrients and vitamins for the development of their body and mind. Heat stress also affects fruit and vegetable production in tropical regions of the world of which some African countries are a part of. This means that children born in such areas of the world will be at risk of nutrient and vitamin deficiency.

This is not good news for children across the world. How could we rob them of their livelihoods due to environmental negligence? How are they supposed to feed their children in the unstable planet we are trying so hard to bequeath to them? But the story does not have to end on a sad note for the future of our species. Key stakeholders must act holistically and in unity to improve the productivity, profitability, and sustainability of crops.

We can make better decisions on land management and utilisation with climate centred data which are thankfully available. We can reduce agriculturally based greenhouse gases' emissions by strengthening the use of renewable energy. Energy plays a crucial role in producing, storing, and cooking our food, and it plays a vital role in food security. About 2.9 billion people depend on inefficient energy systems such as stoves or firewood or dung which releases particulate matter and other polluting gases into the environment for cooking which comes with health risks, social and environmental costs.[60] Today like every other day, millions of women and children will spend hours gathering fuel, cooking indoors, and being exposed to indoor air pollution due to the toxic fumes they breathe in.

Nations must push for the switch to renewable energy, which will improve their countries' overall wellness and the people who live in it and safeguard their children's future. Sometimes, the way we practice agriculture is stuck in the 19th century regarding sustainability and how we manage our natural resources. One other thing could be to empower women since they are key drivers of sustainability in the world. Empowered mothers will raise healthy children.

Combining measures such as efficient production and transportation with the expansion of food choices beyond the three primary grains (wheat, rice and maize) which currently provides for most of our plant-sourced nutrients while reducing food waste will not only improve the chances that children will be better nourished now and in the future. Still, it will also guarantee food system preservation and resilience.

Perhaps the most important prehistoric event that continues to fascinate archaeologists and amateur human geography enthusiasts is Homo sapiens' past mass migration from Africa to the world's different continents. This singular event spurred our species on to ascending the position of global species dominance and arguably becoming the Alpha species. By the time this migration was over, among other competing species such as Homo erectus and Neanderthals, Homo sapiens were the only surviving species for several reasons beyond this book's purview.

However, the point I would like to drive home is the ecological success we have attained over the last 77 000 years as inhabitants of an evolving planet. To put it simply, humans have always migrated for various reasons, including seeking more fertile landmasses; sometimes these mass movements were due to conflict between warring tribes or to flee dangerous environmental catastrophes. As Steven Pinker the Canadian-American science author has put it in his book

Better angels of our nature: why violence has declined, violence has been on the decline for several centuries on end in our world with only 1000 deaths from armed conflicts 2007.[61] If that is true, humans are left with economic and environmental catastrophes as the significant drivers of mass migration for the 21st and 22nd centuries if we sit down with our arms folded and do nothing to reverse climate change and global warming.

But humans are not the only ones who are capable of migrating on the planet. According to experts, the rising temperatures on land and sea are forcing other animal species to move long distances searching for cooler and more favourable habitats. This brings several challenges, none the least, the possibility that these animals can carry several diseases and introduce them to a new environment causing an outbreak that could be of dire health consequences.

One example is Plasmodium (malaria parasite) carrying mosquitoes moving to temperate regions where people might have little or no immunity as these environments warm up. Another consequence of this mass migration is that it could affect food production and distribution networks. Because pests will also move to an environment more favourable to their physiology, countries in the world where these pests are not endemic today, could see a massive cross-border invasion. Already, recently in 2020, the horn of Africa was invaded by dark swarms of locusts which all but blocked sunlight when they swarmed in and feasted on crops in the already arid region. Locusts are known to love areas in which the climate is unpredictable and unstable.

A farmer's cornfield could be reduced to nothing in hours, leading to shortages in cereals' supply, resulting in famines in countries where strong food security policies are not in place. This could threaten food security, lead to mass revolts and instability among populations of humans living in these regions, and displace people as they move for the twin reasons of finding food and seeking safety from physical harm thereby indirectly driving up climate-induced migration.

Some experts have posited that one of our most underrated and wasted human resources; water, could be a reason for conflicts between nations as the continents dry up and get warmer. In fact, water conflicts are not new to the human race and have occurred as far back as 6000 years but could get more pronounced as the climate worsens. But these conflicts are not likely to occur in stable economies. They will most likely happen in already troubled regions of the world where a water conflict will be a secondary reason to draw blood between nation-states. The unavailability of freshwater for fishing, irrigation, and domestic activities could lead to individuals moving towards regions where there is a secure water source. The conflicts that may spin-off from water scarcity could also be a secondary driver of human migration, but not everyone agrees on this point. What do you think? Do you believe that water could become an essential source of conflict and migration in the future?

Experts also disagree on whether people will migrate from poorer to richer countries in what might be an environmentally driven quasi economic migration. Without waiting for these experts' conclusion, people are already beginning to migrate in enormous numbers all the same. People are moving up north towards the Middle East, North America, and Europe from Southeast Asia to escape irregular monsoons and from the dry areas of Africa in what seems like a repeat of humans' great mass migration. But this is only the beginning. This will lead to a lot of demographic changes in the world as we know it today. On whether the world is ready for that, time will tell.

Whatever the case, we need to prepare for the worst-case scenarios and put systems in place to accommodate these populations and demographic changes in the next 50 years while together combating climate change through lifestyle changes and sustainable economic and industrial policies. It is an open secret that migration can be an excellent opportunity for migrants themselves and economies that host them.

Most of the developed world is inhabited by an ageing population and welcoming children and their families into these countries will positively affect the economy and social welfare particularly as more people are needed to care for the aged. Perhaps this is a bit of idealistic thinking because countries could still decide to shut their borders against the flood of climate migrants arriving at their doorsteps, but this would be a slow and silent Auschwitz with populist governments and anti-migrant backlash playing accomplices as the environment pulverises people in nations with a climate disadvantage. In the light of all the information available, we must all prepare for the future because it is coming one microsecond a moment and at an average of 0.17°C (0.31°F) every decade, and with it the future of every child currently alive in the world and those that will be born tomorrow in the way of imminent jeopardy.

Pastoral systems are also very vulnerable to climate change, and it will change the way we go about this form of agriculture and threaten peace and livelihoods as has already been observed in many parts of sub-Saharan Africa. According to the Intergovernmental Panel on Climate Change, pastoralism is practised in about a third of the world's countries by approximately 500 million people, including nomadic communities like the Fulani ethnic group in Nigeria and in many parts of West Africa, agro-pastoralists, and transhumant herders. Due to a panoply of several factors such as land tenure and thinning of arable land, conflicts are not uncommon in these areas between pastoralists and traditional farmers.

The Fulani's as an ethnic group have a relatively large, wealthy, and widely spread population spanning Africa's expanse, including Nigeria, Gambia River, the Volta area of Ghana, and Chad. These herdsmen were restricted to the desert boundaries in the past, but during the twentieth century, they began to migrate and settle in different zones formerly impossible for them to do.[62] This was primarily driven by the desertification of many parts of West Africa due to the Sahara desert's biting winds which consumed anything green and fertile in its way. This, unfortunately, led to conflicts between herdsmen and farmers as far back as 1968 due to the inability to reach a consensus of land sharing. The farmers felt slighted and oppressed as their crops were fed upon by cattle and other smaller herbivores while the herdsmen thought that a fair deal needed to be cut to ensure their livestock's survival. The approach they took was seasonal migration between different regions of Nigeria to pursue green pasture and water. In the rainy season, they stayed up north and let their flock graze on the available grass and herbs while during the long dry seasons, they moved southwards where the land remained green, and the rains still fell.

Most Nigerian adults can recount their childhoods with vivid images and sights of these signature herdsmen, scantily dressed, spurting a rod to guide their flock, and sometimes holding a machete in case they came across wild animals in the forests during their nomadic journeys.

Climate change, unfortunately, does not affect any one group of humans. It also pushes farmers to expand their territory as they search for fertile lands for their crops. When herdsmen do the same for their animals, these often lead to conflicts between these two groups. For years, farmer-herder conflicts have affected the economic livelihood in West Africa taking a toll on children, women, and men as peace is threatened. In March 2010, the sad news reached the world that about 200 people, mostly children, were killed in a Dogo Na Hauwa village in Plateau State, Nigeria. The world saw images of children's heads split into two with machetes and their houses burnt. Later, it was confirmed that these attacks were carried out by Fulani herdsmen on a revenge mission.

What people thought at the time was that the killings were due to the religious crisis that has bedevilled the state since 2001. Well, I still do not know the answer to that to this day. I was moved emotionally beyond words seeing the photos of those children who were mostly under five years old, some of them not yet weaned. I remember even seeing a picture of a foetus harvested from a pregnant woman and left on the ground. I could not believe my eyes or that any human could do that to a fellow human. But the world has taught me better.

When humans compete for resources which seem scarce, the devil is awakened in them, and they can go to any length to prove a point to mark their boundaries and ensure the survival of their own children and kinsmen. But is this the lesson we want to leave our children? That in the face of environmental threats and scarcity of natural resources, we should make it a point of duty to kill other humans who are also trying to survive instead of facing the root cause of the matter which is climate change itself? Isn't this a little bit dystopian or at best Orwellian? I fear for such a world where in order to feed our children or ourselves, we must spill the blood of another human. The climate-induced farmer-herdsmen conflicts have enormously increased recently in Nigeria and have become more sophisticated in casualties and in the manner of hit and run executions. In the last ten years since the attack on Dogo Na Hauwa village by Fulani-herdsmen, more than 35 serious conflicts have ensued with the global terrorism index reporting about 800 direct deaths linked to the farmer-herdsmen conflict in Nigeria as of the year 2015. The victims are mostly children.

Although no evidence currently links it to climate change, plastic pollution is an environmental problem that affects children since they are still at a physiological developmental stage in life. No discussion about the environment in the 21st century should exclude covering the cogent topic of plastic pollution. As a result of human socioeconomic activity since the industrial revolution which gave rise to cheap and convenient packaging and parcelling using plastics, the world's oceans, lakes, rivers, and lands are now littered with 8.3 billion tons of non-biodegradable plastic that poses a threat to the health of children and adults in the world in unprecedented ways. In plastic pollution, no single region of the world is spared due to plastic products' buoyancy and durability. With plastic pollution, two major classes of chemicals related to plastics beg for attention about human health and children's health, particularly concerned phthalates, and bisphenols. Both of them are endocrine-disruptor compounds with bisphenol having estrogenic activity. Being exposed to these chemicals during critical periods of development can pose detrimental effects on children's health. The chemicals easily leach out from plastic and penetrate human skin through personal care and household products or enter the body through other routes from food packaging.

The practicality and convenience plastics provide, are reasons for their ubiquitousness in the human environment. These two chemicals emanating from plastics have been shown to affect the immune system by overstimulating some antibodies' release at least in mouse model research endeavours leading to diverse disease disorders like asthma, dermatitis and rheumatoid arthritis among others in children. This is due to hypersensitivity or prostrate, endometrial, ovarian, breast, cervical, lung and other forms of cancer in the future following neonatal exposure.[63] The National Geographic published an article in 2020 in which they claim that the amount of plastic trash that flows into the oceans every year is expected to nearly triple by 2040 to 29 million metric tons.[64] The cost of a complete overhaul of business as usual when it comes to how we humans deal with plastics runs to over 600 billion US dollars. Global population growth and its demand for plastic are reasons for the upsurge in plastic pollution predicted if we do nothing about it threatening life forms in our planet's water bodies. Almost everyone on the internet today has seen a video of a straw or plastic "necklace" painfully removed from a turtle or fish.

When you consider that these are only rare exceptions since we cannot capture and release all ocean animals, one begins to wonder how deeply rooted this problem really is. The use of plastics can be reduced significantly if we teach people, especially children about the harmful effects of plastics. Eliminating the unnecessary production of plastics, composting, swapping plastic shopping bags which seem to be popular in Africa for paper bags, and reusing containers to mention a few, are some steps that could be taken to curb this catastrophic menace. A study by the German Environment Ministry and the Robert Koch Institute found plastic by-products in almost 100 percent of blood and urine samples from 2,500 children tested between 2014 and 2017. Supposing this data can be extrapolated to all children living around the world and in the light of the dangers of these microplastics, isn't this a ticking time bomb waiting to explode in the future?

Both politics and religion could be the death of any efforts to reverse climate change. On the contrary, both can also become great tools to combat climate change if we tell ourselves the truth and allow science to lead the way.

A US republican congressman expressed his disbelief in humans' efforts to fix climate change and secure the environment in a way that makes clear the kind of thinking that is dangerous to any efforts aimed at positively impacting the environment. This, in a few words, expresses my reservations about religion inspired politics and how it can cheat the world's children of their birth right to a green planet. The Michigan congressman, Tim Walberg once said during a town hall meeting that he believed climate change was real but did not think it was something humans should worry about fixing because it is not our responsibility. As he put it, "I believe there's climate change. I believe climate change has been there since the beginning of time. Do I think man has some impact? Yeah, of course. Can man change the entire universe? No. Why do I believe that? Well, as a Christian, I believe that there is a creator in God who is much bigger than us. And I am confident that, if there is a real problem, He can take care of it."[65] Take a moment to analyse his thoughts on this evidently urgent matter.

In spite of all the negative impacts humans have had on the environment, which is change in itself and thus means that we could definitely make change in the positive direction of the scale, he absolves humanity of any responsibility for climate change and throws the responsibility of correcting all the results of our greenhouse gases' emissions, our ozone layer depleting chemicals, and outright environmental pollution to a Supreme Being. You think his thinking is a rare case? Well, you need to visit Nigeria, where people are ultra-religious to realise that he is not alone in his thinking. Billions of humans think that way due to the influence of religion.

Before the appearance of science on the scene, religion had always been the only succour humanity had in the face of overwhelming catastrophe. And despite all the progress of the 21st century, this still remains the case for many humans.

Blowing wishes on shooting stars I call it. That is where their minds are stuck. While scientists and policymakers seek solutions to these problems to ensure that we bequeath a safe and habitable planet to the world's children, religion imbibes a carefree attitude to the world's environment spurred by the falsely satisfying paradigm of an apocalyptic end of life on Earth. This type of thinking closes the door to all reasonable negotiations and critical thinking that could be ideally tested on the environment's issue by any human who is a true adept of his religious creed.

After much blame-shifting and failure to take responsibility, to combat climate change and global warming, world leaders signed the famous Paris agreement which came into force in November 2016 with the promise to keep global warming well below 2 degrees Celsius or preferably 1.5 degrees Celsius compared to pre-industrial levels which require economic and social transformation to positively impact the environment in the present and in the future using the best available science. The US and China, the two biggest emitters of greenhouse gases, were signatories to this legally binding treaty to the relief of many in the world.

Countries like Turkey, Iran, and Yemen failed to ratify the

agreement mostly because of commitment issues since signing the treaty was a call to climate action that involved changes in the signatories' current socioeconomics. Some countries felt that climate change is not their responsibility since they were not part of the industrial revolution that swept across much of Europe and North America and think that the signing of any agreement is economic suicide and a betrayal of their nationalist goals.

But the world was not ready for what would happen next. In 2019, the former US President Donald Trump initiated the process to pull his country out of the Paris climate treaty, which took effect in November 2020 because he doubted that greenhouse gas emissions could lead to dangerous global warming levels. Before him, President Obama had committed the US to a 28 percent reduction in yearly greenhouse gas emissions by 2025.

The US position under President Trump could lead to the release of more greenhouse gases into the atmosphere for at least a decade if it is not overturned by President Joe Biden. Immediately after taking office, it seems Trump's sole goal was to reverse all his predecessor's legacies including those on environmental issues. In 2017, he ordered the Environmental

Protection Agency to cancel the Clean Power Plan (an Obama-era policy which aimed to cut US emissions from power generation by 32 percent with the deadline of 2030). That alone could be responsible for up to 624 million metric tons of greenhouse gas emissions by 2035.[66]

If religion can stall progress on the environment due to its eschatological teaching, it can also be a cog in the wheel of environmental progress. It depends on what is preached from the pulpit. Coming from the dark ages when Giordano Bruno proposed his cosmological theories that stars were distant suns surrounded by their own planets which could possibly harbour life for which he was tried for heresy by the Roman Catholic Church in 1593 and was burnt at the stake, the Catholic Church has made great progress in its acceptance of science even if there is still a lot that requires debate and possibly changes in fundamental beliefs that are not aligned with reality. I still think that there has been lots of progress since the 16th century.

The Catholic Church has sustained its interest in science by having its own astronomy observatory in what I view as accepting reality and the scientific truth of the day. It is not surprising then that Pope Francis developed a climate encyclical, an authoritative church teaching on the environment and climate change which aims to shape the discussion on these topics. The encyclical addresses the threats to food production as a result of irresponsible fishing and reminds readers of the reasons why migrants are forced to flee poverty especially due to environmental degradation. In the document, the Pope offers a salient corrective to the past theological interpretations I have mentioned in this chapter that states that God gave humanity dominion over the Earth. He challenges the widespread belief patterns that humanity should be at the center-stage of life with regards to the Earth's future and reminds the world of the failures of politicians, big businesses, and big meetings.

The sad but symbolic thing I think however is that Pope Francis handed over a copy of his encyclical to President Donald Trump when he was visited by the President at his residence in the Vatican.[67] Although symbolic, it would have been better if he handed it over to a team of scientists from the US' National Academy of Sciences. It would have meant that the church was forming an alliance with science rather than politics because although religion and science seem to have always been sworn enemies, and politics is still slow to catch up with science, the alliance between science and religion will have more environmental impact to correct the flawed environmental thinking that people have around the world. Religion wields a lot of influence globally, even more than politics in people's lives worldwide. Political action, while necessary, might not be the only solution to climate change.

What does this all mean for children of the world today? The truth is that they cannot wait for us to provide the solutions for such a climate emergency in the light that we fail to act on their behalf. Already, children across the world have joined several campaigns calling for better environmental policies with the goal of securing the environment and safeguarding their future. After winning an essay competition on climate change in a local newspaper in 2018, the young Swedish teenager Greta Thunberg, began protesting at the Swedish parliament building to bring the Swedish government to meet its carbon emissions target agreed by Swedish and other world leaders in the Paris climate treaty. She continued her efforts by missing school every Friday and issued an SOS call on young students worldwide to do the same.

Support gradually grew for her cause, and her protests went viral on social media leading to demonstrations by over 20 000 students in countries like the US, Japan, Australia, Belgium,

The United Kingdom and other European countries. She put her words to practice by choosing to travel by train to limit her gas emissions contribution as she attended these protests. She travelled by yacht to attend a UN climate conference where she made a chilling phenomenal call on the conscience of world leaders by saying; "You have stolen my dreams and my childhood with your empty words. How dare you? I shouldn't be up here.

I should be back in school on the other side of the ocean, yet you all come to us young people for hope. How dare you." Today, she calls for big businesses, banks, and governments to cease investing and subsidising fossil fuels, and instead invest their money in sustainable green technology. The solutions we seek for energy generation are not farfetched, and we do not always have to do something entirely new. It may be time for the world to explore safe nuclear energy by ensuring that it is safely deployed and maintained if we are to meet the energy demands of the future in an environmentally friendly way while combating environmental damage caused by fossil fuels. Greta has inspired many in the world as far as the environment, and climate action is concerned both young and old say a lot about world climate governance, especially regarding how world leaders and adults have abdicated their duty to the environment. In Africa, youths like Oladosu Adenike from Nigeria, Yola Mgogwana from South Africa and Nkosi Nyathi from Zimbabwe are taking centre stage in calling for better environmental policies from their governments and world leaders. I think that there is a global climate revolution silently going on among young people globally, and that may be what could save the world from utter environmental degradation.

For me, I do not think I have done as much as I see children do for the environment in our world today. As a blossoming teenager, I would ride my bicycle in the hilly environs of Vom, a quiet suburb with a beautiful landscape in Jos, Nigeria, and stare at the sky every now and then wondering when the light would go off in the world, and a red cross or some other mysterious object would appear in the blue sky.

I lived in this false reality for several years while also delving into the world of science through books which my friends exchanged with me. At that age, the wrestle between truth and lies, between objective reality and a subjective reality which was probably created to give hope to humans, resulted in a tense battle within me which I never shared with anyone. My only solace was in the innumerable questions that I would ask to the chagrin of much older people. In my first encounter with biological science, I remember asking the teacher who was teaching us reproduction whether it was possible to pass urine and semen during sex. I can still remember the glow and then laughter on my teacher's face. The rest of the class roared in laughter, and from that day, I earned the nickname "rabbit ears" because my new friends thought that I was really listening. My teacher then patiently explained how these biological organs work, and my respect for him grew since that day. No question was too stupid enough to ask my science teacher, and he inspired me to spend time brewing more questions. I had learnt from him that questions were the keys that could free humanity from self-inflicted bondage and open free doors of illumination to everyone.

In today's world, I wish that this free gift is available to everyone, especially children. No one will ask the questions you harbour in your mind. You must ask those that are willing to share objective truth with you until you get to the point where you are armed with the rest of your unanswered questions, you interrogate nature to discover its pleasurable hidden secrets which it bestows only on the curious.

The most important possession we share- the biosphere, has

been under threat since humans left their caves thousands of years ago. Humans contribute to the health of the planet and also its wealth through our daily activities. This time, rather than continuing this spate of nonchalant destruction of life, we have to take control of where our planet is headed by reflecting on the past errors that we have made. Many of us think that the Earth is reshaped for our dwelling. We forget that human activities have forged crevices on our piece of rock within the solar system, we had made forests sprout when our motivation was high, but we have also neutralised acres of natural forests in search of dwelling or wealth. In a way, the Earth is a living organism, and while we frustrate it with our activities, we should remember that it is the only place we can stand on two feet and breathe whatever fresh air we can get.

If you think of the planet as your mother, it might help you to pay more respect to it and reduce the destruction that we are the architect of. I am not condemning all human activities and painting us all rotten. Some activities are necessary for our survival, and the Earth is replete with resources to recover and cater to us all if we are not too greedy. I am intolerant to the industrial scale with which we churn out products we do not need emanating from the insatiable greed that has been kick-started just like in Dante's inferno. If the Earth survives until the sun goes off like a grilled light bulb, every human must understand how it works; this is no two-way equation. We get the results of our activities on Earth as clean and healthy cities and villages, or we get puke-inducing industrial housing estates which leaves us "happy" in the little cages that we call our homes while we sidestep, turn a blind eye, and wear a face mask to avoid the pollution that stinks from around us. We only ought to do the right things always as custodians of the planet.

If everything goes well, the following years should emphasise a clean green Earth as the contrary is really becoming unbearable for many nations, especially in emerging economies where the battle is multifaceted. These countries need all the support that can be offered to boost their awareness and action on maintaining our one beautiful planet in order to secure the future of the world's children.

CHAPTER

10

CRIME, CHILDREN, AND THE DEATH PENALTY

---

*"Many that live deserve death. And some that die deserve life. Can you give it to them? Then do not be too eager to deal out death in judgement."- **J.R.R. Tolkien.***

Every now and then, our attention is caught by the tabloids, or we find ourselves glued to the TV as news seeps in of crimes committed in our cities. We listen in more closely to ensure that its far away from our dwelling and that the crime in question has not affected anyone we know. The reporters capitalise on their story-telling skills and make sure to not leave any gory detail out of the story as they hope to sell more newspapers and grab your attention as you watch your TV. As you watch the news this evening, however, the story of the crime being narrated is not usual. It involves a 15-year-old boy called Hamisu in faraway Zambia, and the child is the lord of violence this time. You learn that Hamisu killed two of his stepsisters with a pair of scissors after which he burnt their bodies in an inferno that engulfed the family home, burning everything to ashes. His father had travelled to Zanzibar to meet with a business partner.

Hamisu's mother had died when he was only five years due to an infection with Hepatitis B that got out of control. His father soon married his stepmother. Since then, Hamisu showed signs of psychological disturbance and violent tendency, which all went unattended to by his busy parents. The camera rested on a woman, his stepmother lying on the floor, unable to stand due to shock from the whole experience of losing two children in one day at the hands of the third. Police try to gather evidence from the crime scene while Hamisu sits behind a pickup vehicle bound like a wild animal. A few months later, after long debates in the courtroom, he is sentenced to three years in the juvenile correction centre after which he will face capital punishment by hanging on his 18th birthday.

I have good news to share. The details of this story, as I have depicted, did not happen as I have described. The sad thing is that almost every day in different countries, crimes like these or worse are perpetrated by children below the age of responsibility and more frequently than should be the case. As innocent as they can be, for some children, besides being victims of crime themselves, they can also be on the other side of the barrel as perpetrators of crime and violence. What's more? Underage children get sentenced for a wide array of crimes or worse, face the gallows in some countries where the death penalty is part of the criminal justice system. The number of incarcerated children worldwide is not known due to poor record-keeping. Still, it is a serious problem to consider as far as the future of children is concerned. The Unicef estimates that over 1 million children are being held behind bars in the world.

Among the world's industrialised economies, the United States has the highest number of children in detention with about 155 000 children in both adult jails and juvenile detention centres.[30] Some years ago, the Human Rights Watch reported that many adults convicted as children continue to be held under pending death sentences while a similar trend involving almost 200 adults on death row in Iran who were sentenced for crimes they committed as children. Although the list of countries which sentences children to death for various crimes continues to dwindle with efforts from organisations like Amnesty International and the Human Rights Watch, as of 2010, countries which had passed a death sentence on children included Iran, Pakistan, Egypt, Maldives, Saudi Arabia, Sudan, Yemen, and Sri Lanka.

In the year 2020, in Kano State, North-western Nigeria, a thirteen-year-old boy was served a a ten year prison sentence by a Sharia court that wields jurisprudence over Muslim inhabitants' with the foggy mission of enforcing Islamic laws in the country. The boy's name is Omar Farouk, and his crime was that he used foul language in an argument with his friend in which he was judged to have blasphemed against Allah and Islam as a religion.

The draconian court had earlier sentenced a musician to death for blaspheming against Prophet Mohammed. It seemed that the Sharia judge who passed both sentences on the same day was on a spree to ensure that residents of this city will be gripped by fear and moved into solemn worship of Allah according to the interpretations of the Quran by these enforcers of outright atrophied 7th-century laws. Omar slightly missed the death penalty himself even if his sentencing was unjust and uncalled for.

He was tried and sentenced as an adult because according to the court, he had attained puberty and was an adult under Sharia law. No one cared that Omar's prison sentence was in violation of the Nigerian constitution, the African Charter of the Rights and Welfare of a Child and the International Convention on the Rights of the Child. No one cared to consider that he was only a child and adults get into arguments every day where they swear, and curse, let alone children who naturally have a lot of liberty of will. The strangest thing about this story is that in line with the data that says the number of incarcerated children is unknown, for Omar, the facts of his situation came to the attention of the public only when the lawyer working with the musician who was also sentenced to death came across young Omar in almost the same moment.

Omar's case gained international popularity with the Unicef condemning his immature detention and prison sentence stating that the situation was of a deep concern. Many media outlets carried the news to garner support for Omar and the musician sentenced to death. The Atheist Alliance International also started campaigns to free them and get the best legal help.

In what became shameful for Nigeria as a country, the head of the Auschwitz memorial in Poland, Piotr Cywinski, called for a rethink on Omar's case and volunteered to serve part of the young boy's prison sentence. He called on Nigeria's President Muhammadu Buhari to act with humanity at the back of his mind and salvage the young boy's future. In his strongly worded letter to the president, he said "As the director of the Auschwitz Memorial at the site of the German Nazi extermination camp, where children were imprisoned and murdered, I cannot remain indifferent to this disgraceful sentence for humanity. He should not be subject to the loss of the entirety of his youth, be deprived of opportunities and stigmatised... for the rest of his life."[68] Omar's family was not spared either. His mother had to flee to another State to escape the angry mob that charged at their home when Omar's sentence was passed.

In Nigeria and many African countries, the physical and mental health of detained children suffers extreme hardship and attrition due to the high probability that they will be physically, emotionally, and sexually abused in the jail cells they are being held in either by the adult inmates or by the guards of such correctional facilities. Sexual assault is a crucial issue for both boys and girls who are detained with adults. Incarcerated children also miss out on a structured educational process that could help them realise their potential, primarily when they are held as a risk for national security or immigration reasons.

[30]By deporting migrant parents of children at the Mexico-US border, and detaining the children, thereby separating them from their parents, former US President Donald Trump catalysed a chain reaction of suffering in the children that were being held in what has become a classic case in which the world was able to follow the effects of incarceration in the lives of children almost in real-time. These young children, some of them not even teenagers, had been separated for several years from their parents which led them to suffer from significant mental health issues, with some being suicidal. When the zero-tolerance migration policy of the Trump administration was announced, the world began to see images

of children sleeping in cages and crying for their parents. This provoked far-reaching criticism from within the US and the whole world but nothing much changed for these children.

According to international law, children's incarceration must conform to the law and should be used only as a last resort measure for the shortest period possible. Sadly, most of the children behind bars have been held for protracted periods and have been the victims of abuse, neglect, and degradation of the dignity of their person. The experiences of these children who will be adults tomorrow can turn an angel into a devil before you can say the word 'peace'.

The strange thing is that besides cases like Hamisu's or Omar's, they are held for various reasons that seem flimsy at best. In a world trying to get children to attend school, some children are sent to prisons for missing school, having consensual sex, which was judged to be inappropriate at that age, for having an abortion or for being rude to their parents. Children may also be held in some countries in Africa for same-sex relationships they may have with another child. It is not that some of these examples do not concern me but that I think they should be considered misdemeanours in a child's life and as part of the paths some children will explore before their character solidifies as they become adults. I have stolen pieces of meat from my mother's pot and been rude to her as a teenager, especially on occasions where she tried to prevent me from meeting with girls that I fancied. Should I have also been sent to prison for being a rude pimply teenager? The reality remains that if I had gone to jail for correctional purposes of my 'crimes', I would have come out worse than I went in. And this is precisely what happens to most children when they are incarcerated. The question is not whether children commit crimes or not. Instead, the question should be whether the punishment or retribution is justified for their age and comprehension of the social norms that bind the society they live in together.

To answer these questions, we must first examine the causes of crime among children. Who are or what is responsible for deviant behaviour in children which drives them to commit an act recognised by their society as a crime, causing them to be incarcerated? It's a cycle But to solve the problem, we must first decipher the process. Although children are usually victims of the system and the society's interpretations of justice, as I have mentioned earlier, they can also be the perpetrators of crime themselves. Research and experience gathered by the human species over several centuries show that environmental, social, and biological factors can lead a child to commit a crime.

It has always ticked researchers and social observers' interest if child abuse could make children more crime-prone. Just like a dark curtain that blocks the beautiful rays of the sun from getting into a house and bringing life to everything that it touches, in the same light, child abuse or maltreatment prevents children from leading an everyday life and blossoming. There is evidence that many adult criminals were abused in childhood, and children who commit crimes are likely to be suffering or have suffered some form of domestic or external abuse. In the United States, 9 out of 1000 children in the welfare system have suffered abuse.

In the world, being neglected is the most common form of abuse suffered by children followed by physical abuse, emotional abuse and sexual abuse. Abuse in childhood has some obvious consequences in the life of a human which come up later in life and show up as difficulties in accomplishing academic feats and problems with being economically stable in the society without mentioning the physical and emotional turmoil that they have to go through which may last their entire lives. What has usually slipped under the radar for most social scientists is how abuse in childhood is associated with crime. But we now know that children who have experienced abuse, neglect or maltreatment in childhood are more likely to engage in socially abhorrent behaviours later in life like theft or violent crimes. Using complex statistical models in the US, international development and child expert, Dr Hannah Lantos and her colleagues examined data of over ten thousand individuals representing the US's entire adolescent population to answer two questions.

First, they wanted to see the relationship between childhood abuse and criminal behaviours from adolescence into young adulthood. And secondly, whether the association between childhood abuse and criminal behaviour varied by sex, race or ethnicity and sexual orientation and if so, how?[69]

After examining the data and performing some computations, Dr Lantos and her team found that this association did not vary by race or sexual orientation. However, males who were abused as children were more likely to be engaged in violent crimes in adulthood. One thing to clarify about the work that Dr Lantos did with her team is that this was not a mere prediction model where they were speculating. The data they got from over ten thousand individuals included both information on already committed crimes and instances of abuse suffered during childhood. Basically, they were using their statistical models to match and follow these individuals over time while they ensured to consider other factors that could modify any relationship they were likely to find.

The salient beauty of what they found is that whether children were black or white, African Americans or Hispanic, and no matter their sexual orientation, and no matter what race children were born into; there is not a single variation of race or sexual orientation that child abuse is associated with the future probability to violate the law through misdemeanours or violent crime.

This means that all children and youth on our planet, no matter their race, the ethnicity of sexual orientation respond negatively to child abuse, neglect and maltreatment. Due to the insufficient data-curating culture of African countries, I am not aware of any similar research that has been completed on this matter in the African continent, but I hope that it becomes clear to all of us that all children of the world are affected by abuse which could influence them towards a life of crime. The last word I would use to describe the sentences or punishments that these children get is 'justice'. There is no justice for the African child. The African child is pressed on every side. Who will rescue the world's bastion of hope?

Many children and pregnant women have been exposed to dangerous levels of the element lead. These children and pregnant women come into contact with it from lead-based paints at home or in schools, household products, mining and smelting operations, petrol, soil, dust, drinking water or only from the outdoor air. The point is that the chances of being exposed to lead are high, especially several years ago.

The risk of exposure to this element also differs depending on which country you put under the lens. The primary source of direction is different for each region of the world. In Nigeria, the kind of lead exposure that has caught the local and international community of experts' attention is exposure from artisanal gold mining activities and from lead dust in the environment. Many populations across the world have therefore been exposed to it. In Nigeria, little is done to reduce the chances of lead exposure in children. There is a popular hypothesis or school of thought which keeps being tested; it says lead is linked to aggressive crime since even at low levels of exposure, it can lead to anti-social behaviour. Why this hypothesis is still under debate by some policymakers at the helm of affairs despite the overwhelming evidence from several studies proving that exposure to this toxic element in childhood even at moderate levels could lead to criminal behaviour later in adulthood is perplexing.

In 2016, some scientists in Australia tested this hypothesis in a cardinal endeavour to understand the problem's dynamics. They investigated the rates of assault rates of impulsive and aggressive crimes over time and compared this with concentrations of lead in the air in the several suburbs of New South Wales, examining the data closely from 24 years earlier using computerised crime data and pollution data from air monitoring sites in the region. Although their study did not imply a causal association in the strict sense, they found that lead in the air was responsible for 30% of future impulsive and aggressive crimes.

[70]Through this, they proved that there was a strong association between lead exposure and the rates of aggressive crimes that followed in New South Wales. This has implications for children worldwide, especially in Africa where such studies are rarely designed, not to talk of using the findings to change

national and regional policies. It means that many African children are blindly at the mercy of lead and other toxic metals as the imperfect criminal justice system prevails over their lives. We need to act for the children of the world by taking measures to prevent exposure to lead and other environmental contaminants which have consequences in a child's neurodevelopment and can make the difference between serving jail time, facing the death penalty, or living a fulfilled life.

In his book Free Will, neuroscientist, author, and philosopher, Sam Harris recounts a true story of two criminals who break into a sleeping man's house. One of the criminals ends up bludgeoning the sleeping man to a pulp with a baseball bat before binding his hands despite the poor man's screams in a way that seemed like he enjoyed the suffering of the poor man.[71] He did not stop there as his brain's pleasure centre was getting more activated.

He drove for several miles to the gas station with the poor man's wife and bought several gallons of gasoline after which he drove to the bank and withdrew her savings. On returning to the house, he raped and strangled her to death. You can read more about this in Harris's excellent book. It might be easy for us to apportion blame on the criminals for their behaviour and condemning them swiftly to the worst punishment we can think of. You could even consider the death penalty when you realise that they set the house ablaze with the man's children still fastened with cords by them to the bed. The poignant question that Harris wanted his readers to ask and which I consider and ask myself since the question of justice began to trouble me is whether these criminals acted out of free-will. It would interest you to know that one of them was abused as a child while the other had some pre-existing conditions. I have found it challenging to define free will. This has convinced me that free will doesn't exist per se even if we choose to believe so. At best, it is an illusion that we choose to live with to have structure and function in the world.

Harris says, "Either our wills are determined by prior causes, and we are not responsible for them, or they are the product of chance, and we are not responsible for them." So, which one is it?

Besides sociological explanations of crime, biology is being used to explain the tendency to commit a crime. Aspects of human nature such as genetics and neurological reservoirs of individuals can distinguish criminals from non-criminals in a sample of humans, whether they are Africans, Europeans, Asians, or Americans. Forensic scientists and neuroscientists often investigate the prefrontal cortex of the brain, the central nervous system, neurotransmitters like serotonin, and hormones like testosterone which are believed to influence crime.

The prefrontal cortex is said to be the brain section that is responsible for higher-level cognitive processes like decision-making, attention, regulating emotions, and controlling impulses. Scientists have observed structural and functional deficits in the way the prefrontal cortex is organised among criminals and people with behaviours that can be termed 'anti-social'.

[72]This basically means that undergoing structural or functional damage to this part of the brain for any reason and at any point in the developmental stage of childhood would put such individuals at risk of attempting crime and violence. This slight difference between two children would mean that one of them is predestined for a life of crime if nothing is done about it while the other will be considered by society as a gentleman-both of them, through no dedicated, conscious

effort on their part. This is not to say that people are not responsible for their behaviour. It would be catastrophic if society functioned under that paradigm. However, take the case of individuals who have undergone a lobotomy, for example, a surgical technique in which part of the brain is removed, such as is used to treat extreme cases of epilepsy. Many people who undergo such surgeries report that they experience a personality change and begin to do and enjoy certain things that they did not formerly enjoy or find that they stop some idiosyncrasies altogether.

Since the Human Genome Project was completed in 2003, many gene areas responsible for alcoholism, mental health issues, and so on have been mapped out and are now under scientists' studious lenses. It is not surprising that whether genes exist that predispose people to a life of crime was revisited by several researchers interested in the subject.

While it is difficult to argue that one single gene codes for criminal behaviour, it is not out of place to argue that the interaction of several gene blocs, their expression catalysed by environment could make a child born into a stable, loving family resort to crime even when there are no other causal factors. The alternative of a crime-free life of prosperity is available. I must caution here, however, the attribution of every crime to genetic factors. Genetic factors alone do not determine if a child will take the low path of crime. The expression of these gene segments is usually mediated by the environment. A child with these genes raised in a loving family has a strong likelihood of escaping crime while another child with the same set of genes raised in a hostile and toxic family could be triggered into criminality. In molecular genetics, it is known that a gene related to the serotonin system may be associated with the recurrence of alcoholism and violent behaviours. When we look at a criminal, we would then judge him for his harmful acts but forget that what lies beneath the skin speaks volumes.

Evidence also exists that higher testosterone levels could be obtained from the blood of prisoners who have committed violent crimes or in people with aggressive behaviour.[73] From an evolutionary standpoint, these aggressive tendencies are behavioural residues from our distant ancestors determined by testosterone. It is difficult to observe this kind of testosterone-determined violence happening on a large scale in children or in the adult population simply because violent behaviours determined by testosterone are inhibited by social upbringing. Beginning from the embryonic stage of life, testosterone begins its action on the destiny of a child. Yet again, the expression of violent behaviour is determined by the expression testosterone receptor gene. In 2014, some researchers performed an experiment in which they measured foetal testosterone levels. Matching the results with criminality, they found that increased foetal testosterone levels were moderately correlated with the likelihood of committing various crimes in both men and women.

[74]So before a child is born, a lot has already been naturally put in place that influences the violent thoughts, bodily arousal, and brutal acts of violence that an individual child may commit. Predestination, however, is not destiny as far as the science of criminology goes. Children and families can still build a crime-free life through social structures such as social services and government units. For example, even though height is not evenly distributed in the human population, nutritional interventions have resulted in humans' average height improving over time. This same kind of thinking could be applied to crime prevention.

The time has come for the discussion to focus less on parenting style and peer groups' influence on other factors that can explain crime and the trajectory of crime in life.

Today, each time I hear of a criminal act, I wonder if the criminal was abused in childhood, exposed to toxic metals in childhood or has some biological anomaly, leading to his propensity to a life of crime. This does not mean that excuses have to be made for all criminals and that people should not take responsibility for their lives and actions. It only means that we need to think of a way to share responsibility as a society given that crime can have a broad effect on all of us. As the criminal justice systems in Africa and many emerging countries struggle to control crime that starts from juvenile delinquency, it would make both economic and social sense when decision-makers consider the role of biology in crime. After all, this is the 21st century.

After examining your conscience with the facts on how environment, biology and social factors can influence a child's probability of committing a crime and given that society falls short in fulfilling a child's needs. Can you say that there is justice in the death penalty, especially when served upon a child? Life is precious whether it's the life of animals such as gazelles, flamingos, gorillas, mice or that of humans. Once life is snuffed out of a living being by any means, it becomes impossible to reverse this process. It results in death. Human dignity should not allow for humans to be executed for any reason-simple. Every execution throws a cloak of guilt on the rest of us who spectate while a fellow being is lethally neutralised under the auspices of the law or outside of it and it makes us less dignified than a jury of hyenas. Most death penalty sentences are for homicides but one death can never balance out another; even when one of these deaths is implemented by the state. Therefore, state-sanctioned murder in the name of justice is, in reality, the worst form of injustice that humankind has been able to come up with since we decided to live under the law.

In many parts of the world, the needs of children are often neglected. Indeed, many people see them as members of society who occupy the government's social agenda's lowest echelon. As a result, they are exploited and what concerns them is not taken seriously. Yet they are the ones who will become the adults of tomorrow.

Indeed, at the level of governance, the mentality is not so different. But in everyone, citizens, and great politicians, we are all guilty, either in the past or the present, but never in the future. The long-awaited upheaval must begin within us, with us and around us. The phenomenon of neglected children resulting in criminality is a global problem, but it is in full swing in emerging economies. However, the burden of this social challenge is not something to be left on the shoulders of one individual: not for pain or glory but for the dignity of children and human beings on our planet. Everybody in my country and all my friends and world citizens that I have had the opportunity to meet in my life have shown me that if we work together, we can change this misconception.

I also know that it is not only in Africa that this problem of juvenile crime exists. We need to help each other to be able to deal with the battle for livelihood all over the world for several reasons. The more time I spend with the children and ask them questions, the more I feel happy to know that there is hope, given the quality of life that awaits us somewhere in the future and that crime may in fact be reduced. It is up to us to decide whether we want to remain in the dilemma of applying the death penalty (or other harsh judgement on children). I belong to the school of thought that advocates crime prevention by building a world where justice and peace reigns, starting with winning childhood first.

Who is responsible for the final outcome of the character of a criminal who has already been convicted, or better still, what end does the world expect from the death of a criminal?

These are all questions that will remain forever in my mind. This is not really something new, but we know that society is an integral part of these condemned citizens' attributes. So, if the display of the noble path in our world is to begin, it will start with you and then the great politicians of Africa and ultimately our world. It is about stopping injustice because we know that injustice practised anywhere is injustice everywhere, especially in our globalised world since we reap what we sow.

The justice I am talking about is the realisation of the right to life set out by world governments for every human in several conventions: for example, the Universal Declaration of Human Rights in 1948. In this case, it serves mostly abandoned children in the streets who will get involved in petty crimes while searching for life basics. These crimes will grow like an avalanche and with a high chance will arrive at a capital crime. And then ultimately the death penalty?

Another thing that is not new is that everyone is born with inalienable human rights, including the right to life. This right began the day the first humans evolved on our planet. Therefore, the abolition of the death penalty is not something new, and it is not a gift. There will be no need for it if we work hard to prevent crime in children. In short, it is wiser to have fun and to direct energy from the application of capital punishment towards crime prevention. It's really cheaper to create a law-abiding citizenry starting in childhood than to use what we think are painful measures to control crime. It is counter-intuitive but worth considering.

Should we do nothing in the face of injustice and offer our necks to the masters of death from the four corners of the planet? Every day, still in our modern world, people find themselves on death row for forgivable offences and even for the little mistakes they have made in leading their lives. If not in Saudi Arabia, it would be in the United States - two highly developed countries where the death penalty is still in force, or it could be in a remote part of the world. This is not the time to be a spectator of the struggle to abolish this inhuman practice.

The world needs you to play a role to reverse this shameful practice and put it in the dustbin of history where it belongs. Despite my worry about this subject, two-thirds of the world's countries have abolished the shameful practice, but why not the others? There is no justification for condemning to death or executing others under the guise of pursuing justice. Justice is at odds with the death penalty practice; for when justice seeks to establish peace, the death penalty sets up a bloody war - the war of hearts. Human beings who can no longer show kindness to others. I am not saying today that we should forgive all criminals, but what I am saying instead is that they should have the opportunity to change their opinions and behaviours by having time to think about it in prison rather than using the same instrument they wield to kill them.

There is no evidence that the application of the death penalty is reducing crime in the world. But we know that the humanitarianism of the parties involved in human affairs raises living standards, establishes friendship, brotherhood among men, and helps carve the path of human life on earth towards utopia and ultimately towards actualising a near-perfect system of justice.

Some people say that a perfect system of justice in the world is an illusion and will never happen. Maybe, but I think it is an illusion that is worth pursuing. And it won't be manna from heaven. We have to build it, starting from the grassroots. You can choose any path you like from this question of justice for children held for crime in the world and the risk of the death penalty, but before you do, you have to remember that we always pay for our actions or inactions in life. Therefore, we must know that the pen of the future is in our hands and that we must take the responsibility of writing a beautiful story for the next generations to avoid the filth that surrounds us. The death penalty will be unnecessary if we win childhood first. Let's choose the higher path. But am I just a dreamer? The death penalty is not justice and can never be justified. It is the lowest, darkest ebb of human dignity and honour.

Thinking about it all, the question must have crossed your mind, "How do we then deal with juvenile offenders or prevent crime?" This is a valid question to ask given that the reality of crime bites hard, especially as the radius of its location approaches us. If we are to successfully cut down the probability that children would be involved in crime, we must first pay attention to how children are raised.

As is commonly known, children raised with love and care usually turn out to be great individuals without the taint of crime in their lives no matter if they have the genetic risks that would dictate that their lives will be one of catastrophes and crime. Also, at the state level, we must intervene in families lacking good parenting skills and children who show behavioural problems from at least seven years old. Attention should also be paid to single mothers, and it should be the case that in African countries, care for mother and child does not stop after birth. Care and support should be provided to prevent the chances of child abuse. The primary way we can prevent crime in children is by acting early and fast. By not waiting for children to commit crimes so that we can jail them; but by identifying children at risk of crime so that, by providing care and support early enough as they start their lives, a higher path to life can be revealed to them.

Once again, the importance of environmental stewardship comes into focus. To prevent crime resulting from exposure to heavy metals like lead, we must be more concerned about how we treat our environment and be aware of the interrelationships between the environment and humans. For example, decreases in average blood lead levels in pre-schoolers have been linked to dramatic crime reductions and subsequent juvenile arrests for violent crime dropped by as much as a full 50 percent.

[75]Controlling the levels of lead in the environment is an achievable objective and is already on the Sustainable Development Goals agendas that aim to "cut down the

number of illnesses and deaths from hazardous chemicals and air, water and soil, pollution and contamination." Secondly, it also matches the agenda to "achieve environmentally sound stewardship of chemicals and wastes throughout their lifecycle and significantly reduce their release to air, water and soil in order to minimise their adverse impacts on human health and the environment."

Omar Farouk was freed in January 2021 through the efforts of United Nations agencies, the Atheists Alliance international and many individuals from around the world who used all their resources to ensure that he was protected from an unfair criminal justice system. Many more children are not so lucky even when their crime is not a joke about a god. What can we do today to ensure that the future of children like Omar is safe from all forms of tyranny, and injustice?

C H A P T E R

11

THE FUTURE OF AFRICA AND ITS CHILDREN IN THE WORLD

———

"Where children are, there is the golden age."
Novalis

The question 'who is a child or human?' has been a dilemma for a very long time and has held humans in awe for millennia. The mystery of this stage of life is that once the jigsaw puzzle of meaning is almost complete to explain it, one would have outgrown the innocence of childhood. These existential questions have spurred us into remarkable actions that have translated on our historical timeline as both disaster and progress; with our species successfully hovering above the planet's food and power chain. A quick retrospective reflection on our origin and a curious peer through this historical cloud of knowledge into the future reveals one thing: we are slowly but surely unravelling who we are on the sands of time. Being human for now, is not an answer glaringly carved into a rock. By living our lives, we discover who we really are; beasts or guardians of the world; we decide. Be it known at this point, that it is beyond the capability of any single being to thoroughly demonstrate humanness to a child. Being human is a virtue we must weave out together while upholding the obligation to unravel the beautiful corolla of peace, empathy, love, and the sheer willingness to stick together through the vortex that life inevitably pulls us through.

As humans preoccupied with foraging the planet for physiological and emotional satisfaction, it is easy to become preoccupied with these needs that we enclose ourselves in the narrow societal circles that provide the secure stockpiles of these needs. We could thereby ignore the beautiful light of life that summons us beyond the comfort of the social and environmental circles we are familiar with and feel comfortable with. We may forget our obligations to the next generation as we seek to satisfy our needs. Simply put, we may not realise if we are engaged in life as responsible custodians of its ecosystem or as disengaged foragers. We will always hold within our hands the keys to ensuring that life is pleasantly enriching for every child as an individual in the different communities in which we have organised ourselves over millennia. We can effortlessly share not just ideological hope and love, but to feel sympathy and to douse pain by ensuring that we can provide for our physical needs without unduly harming the planet. Beyond the innumerable surprises that our conduct often results in, which of course makes for life's spices and entertaining adventures, this may be what it means to be a human capable of demonstrating humanness to a child.

Events in our development and trajectory have made us almost enchanted with our personal experience of what being human means. We fail to realise that this experience has diverged into an even richer one of collectively sharing and enjoying the natural endowment of belonging to arguably the most successful species on earth. Are we more human when our ego fuels our desires to engage in wars; and ignore hunger and squalor? Or are we more humans when compassion drives us into service that upholds the dignity and sanctity of all life? Is the goal of being human to protect our culture from each other or promote and share cultural diversity? These are not easy questions to answer. More than any other time in our collective history, we are at the threshold of victory for humanity and for the future custodians of the planet. We must press forward together, holding hands into the liberation of enlightenment or dwell in the obscurity of our ignorance. We hope that we can all enjoy and share the universal experience of being human, whether we are children today or adults tomorrow.

Although the natural environment where we live may seem to be reined in by the laws of nature, they are, in fact, fashioned by the workings of the human mind. This part of our being is the birthplace of disaster and of the most delicate forms of virtues. From here, we decide how we treat our children on the planet, how we react to environmental issues that affect their future, or whether we are the engineers of conflict that will destroy them or the emissaries of peace to build them. Every individual human is in control of their mind's offspring, and I strongly hope that beauty in the world and the appreciation of life will continuously flourish because we all take responsibility for the future of the world's children by taking care of them while they look up to us for leadership and guidance because the foundation of the world's future is laid during childhood.

It would be very ironic to begin to view the endless differences between Africa and Europe (an archetype for Western civilisation) through one lens. I have struggled to see them as one, but the difficulty and difference between these two words begin to manifest more and more each time I take a closer and positive look at how much similarities and differences they both have-my Africa and then our Europe.

The wheels of technology and history propelled by both sides of the divide, a conclusion which makes me begin to inspire thought-provoking images within my mind, I haven't seen the light at the end of the tunnel in a way I have since the last time I took a look at these emerging trends inspired by technology in conjunction with history, which has now changed my mindset about what these two have come to represent.

These two different continental shelves, which take root from its geographical location understandably, underscores the delineation of consciousness, which is the significant difference between the two worlds—continents. For want of more definition, I will implore us to view the words of Novalis, "Where children are, there is the golden age" which only recently formed the nucleus with which I have now considered the disparities between humanity and humans. In his life, Georg Philipp Friedrich Freiherr von Hardenberg, who was better known by the pseudonym Novalis, was an 18th-century German aristocrat, poet, thinker, essayist, author, mystic, and an invested philosopher of Early German Romanticism.

Novalis who was born into a somewhat less aristocratic family in ancient Saxon, in his other quote which mirrors the reality of life and thoughts, said "I often feel, and ever more deeply I realise, that fate and character are the same conception". That which makes us manifest more in our self is the most critical aspect of our thought which is everything that defines our collective consciousness as humanity.

Africa is a land of virgin earth, mostly unoccupied and most of its vast rainforest still is under-utilised or not used at all but nonetheless under environmental threat. Unlike most of traditional Europe, we have a growing youth population, a strong presence of humanity and some of the things that could be identified as our weaknesses and strengths, culturally rooted in service and amplified relationships with our fellow humans, we are enshrined to inspire each other, first as individuals and then better still as a collective. What makes us genuinely unique is our most significant threat to existence, our worries of today and the fears of yesterday, our concerns of the future and many more of the several things that need to be addressed on the count as they appear. As with all aspects of human society, we too are hanging in there, doing what we must do to stay alive and keep hope alive.

We haven't fared well, but we haven't managed terribly either. For us, it's not as much as it is about winning or something about not losing, but it's about the genuine connection between our network of souls and body, secured together as with ties unseen, the relationship between humanity is same as the connection between a mother and her young foetus, a reality that all are one and that one is equal to all.

Sadly enough, we haven't seen this trend play out in the same reality as the issues surrounding the failure of leadership or poor governance and the many severe consequences of administrative death in Africa. We have not done enough or better in this regard, but fair enough, these undesirable circumstances are not the only yardsticks with which to begin to measure our soul or our collective consciousness as a people.

There is work to be done, there are several more tasks to handle, and there will be more and more challenges to overcome en route Africa's emancipation of itself from the shackles imposed by foreigners through well-thought-out destructive economic policies and other self-imposed quagmires by Africans, an unfortunate situation in all hue and cry.

We have two different definitions of success, one in which the individual alone gets better, and the most important or meaningful description of it all, a state of consciousness where everyone gets better and equally urges the others to get back better, while it lasts. To us that singular aim clarifies what we are looking at and what it means to be successful, the idea around the individual as against the collective is a significant factor in understanding Africa and what makes it different from Europe.

In Africa, we have a conversation about what we are versus who we have become too. A little more or less like the usual conversation between a grown-up man and his head, where one answers reality-based questions about life, family, work, finances, relationship with religion, friends and the extensive forms of relations which spread through time and time, alongside the lines of both ancestral traditions like paternal and maternal culture.

We have also queried ourselves into the areas of life we in Africa considered sacrosanct in the past areas of thought we felt could inspire the wrath of the spirit of the land. Existential views that involve manifesting a rebellious natural way of inquisition into the world we think exist outside our knowledge but somewhere else in our consciousness, a land any living being would be scared to tread on.

These types of inquisitions were logically considered forbidden in our ancient forms of laws and traditions, Africa was and is mostly considered or believed to be a land of the ancestors of our land, and to be frank and sincere our forefathers and forebears have walked this path for several centuries, spanning thousands of years. It may not be disproportionate to agree that somewhere along the line, the conversation about the African homestead remarked to be the ancestors' land still holds a steady viewpoint.

Interestingly, during this period of thought-provoking images spiralling in my mind, I have since agreed to look forward or beyond the assurances of my immediate environment. In the minds of many, it could be considered a collision of a sort for one to question the many unanswered questions surrounding the unseen realities of this world.

Who in his mind would readily accept the composition of the ancient civilisation around the world we have come to see that what we may say is right can be considered as a realistic viewpoint classical of what our node of existence is capable of, where one is said to be a vision and its merits made unquestionable?

There is a consistency in some viewpoints in Africa, centred around the views of originality and creativity. This particular opinion piece about ourselves is remarkably accurate of what is believed to be the norm, the logical nature of the human mind may not be in agreement, but this can be considered unworthy. No one within this sphere of influence will eventually alter long-held views, which tends to be the most critical truth in this world.

To deepen one's understanding or thoughts on this conversation, it would be said to be true of humans in their rebellious spirit for the exchange to be held in separate ways, a decision which can allow for us to continue in line without the long-held truth be it free or controlled.

Within these events' context stems the now held discoveries of the modern world, the annunciation of a new generation of humans with the tact and drive to sustain a suitable inquisition into this new truth.

The way forward is indeed in everything good about Africa, we are not here to define ourselves so the stranger would appreciate who they imagine us to be. And I am not sure either that the best regards will be on defining ourselves to ourselves in a way that makes us acquire a new meaning, we are who we are, and that is the best possible definition of the African, be it ancient, modern, or ancestral.

Evolution is the greatest thing that happens to every human civilisation, and upon this new generation to speak of consciousness, of a kind never before seen by anyone, not known to strangers, and not even seen by historical watchers. This new edition is the very original thing, which is considered a gradient, which is a measure that illustrates how much we have learnt in our many uncountable years of existence, we have evolved, we have developed, and we have experienced everything and much more than we can ever imagine.

Every civilisation has its own unique problems, Africa was designed with its own flaws. And Africa based on this realisation is held accountable for its own difficulties, like every generation we too have seen what needs addressing. Our own problems also have evolved with us through the years, in many ways as possible, we will continue to aspire to overcome difficulties in as many more ways as possible.

The future of Africa and its children lies in the hands of Africans, knowingly or unknowingly, this new generation has that responsibility, it is a blessing to be responsible for steering the world to a new direction, it would not be easy, but it would not be too hard enough. Learning from past and present mistakes offer the most significant opportunities to correct the past and present errors. Circumstances come and go, sometimes they do not change at all, depending on what is happening within the context but what matters is the need to address the issues surrounding our collective responsibility, the connection to respond to this situation is critical to nature.

No one dares to state otherwise, because doing so would be detrimental to the survival of the African race with all its children, we are defined by the many battles we fight and how much we made of the challenges we emerged from.

There are a lot of different ways to inspire hope in Africa, but most importantly we have to start from today's turmoil. I have not seen otherwise, but I believe everything good will happen eventually for Africa's children and their friends in other regions of the world will see Africa as a land of opportunity and hope. We have come this far, and every consideration about running away, or absconding from the continent should be tossed to the wind. The best way to be emancipated from these shackles imposed on us by ourselves and made possible by the strangers from lands afar is a testament to our resolve to make hay while the sun shines.

Hopefully, the horrors of the past are now behind us, the glorious days of today belong to the future, we must take advantage of this new position to push forward with zest and life, throwing everything we have got back into the contest, fighting against everything known and unknown, bearing in mind that our most tremendous adversity is not the strangers from lands afar alone. Still, our own shadows lurk around us day and night, questioning our resolve to inspire, and underscoring our drive to embrace our fight, the whole new background from which we are meant to liberate. It could be considered our most significant adversity, truth be told, to fight a known enemy can be daunting but to fight an enemy which is oneself can be the ultimate disaster waiting to happen.

Having said these, I will allow room for the next generation of Africans conscious of the individual self, folks with the spirit of the ancient warriors, young people and children with the zest and sight of the hawk, with the courage to continue to the final rounds towards the finish line. However, I have since agreed that in a race, while the finish line may be the last line to victory, in this humanity's race, the finish line will be a stepping stone towards tomorrow's challenges.

We are prepared at least so it seems with the new wave of the African spirit made more possible by the drive to know and seek, which is the inquisition we have since talked about in part and then in whole as the conversation tended to twist and turn following every twist and turn into the final lapse of this conversation, which sadly will continue to spark several occasions of different things both problematic and imagined.

In case you are not aware, there are a new kind of Africans on the block who are; ready to learn, no longer infected with the lies of the past, and no longer inferior or superior to knowledge. These new Africans are prepared with the time and the resolve to seek and enquire, with no holds barred, no areas of thought considerations which would instil the fears of the unknown enemy, the new Africans are seemingly in control of their destiny, armed with the defences of the ancient world, seeking and searching for the humanity long lost to the untold and told lies of the present, a natural history watcher, nursing with every kind of ambition, the young blood ready to sacrifice his comfort and his own life to enquire, even about the ancestors and the history they left behind, majority of them buried alive inside the deepest depths of the earth, in the belief that the truth would never be found.

The dry wells are now being dug, young men and woman with all the time and strength in this world, tilling and digging up the dirt, carving up the earth and prodding deeper and deeper into the earth, where the actual final lines have been tossed into, covered up with sands, we who are now suing for the truth must find peace and that peace shall emancipate our generation from its backwardness.

As days turn into years and as knowledge continues to outgrow our ignorance, the information within our collective disposal continues to outgrow our holding capacity, which we have increased over time as with the demand to store more and more of the information available. We are still looking for answers, we are always seeking the truth, and we are still making the efforts of yesterday's long-lost years to get informed about the reality surrounding our thoughts.

Who else can be called to answer, Africa needs more girls and boys, women, and men capable of making gains in their lives, proving the strangers wrong time after time, and chasing out the spirit of self which is still very much active in our minds despite the many years of effort to get rid of it, we must understand that it's not something that will be easier to handle! Still, we have surely learnt to keep it in a corner where it belongs while doing the same task we set out to do in the first place, seek and inquire, and ye shall find.

Life is not about winning or losing, it is a very complicated process that we all must continuously continue to inspire to seek and find. The work of the history watcher is not just to watch things unfold, and clearly not only to document, but it also embodies everything about us, to seek, to find, to report and to tell the truth about the earth we have evolved from and into, this we must do and these we shall continue to do with all our heart and strength, for it is the only way to get the ultimate goal reached. We shall tell our story from the matter, and we shall not consider ourselves or the strangers, the truth is for everyone similar to the strangers and the spirit of the self which is also an issue around us.

To begin to understand Africa, one needs to start asking those critical questions. What is the context of the conversation surrounding its existence? What is the concept of the Africans all about? What makes it challenging to understand? What makes it different from the others? And why is the subject of Africa still showing up every now and then on a global scale daily? We haven't started yet to talk about its highs and lows. Always, it will be a categorical statement in due time to attempt a definition of Africa we all woke up from our first sleep in, an Africa we grew up in, an Africa which is now more than a collective homeland, a homeland which serves as a home for nearly two billion people, different colours of the same people, same people of other races all unified at least. Hence, it seems to be united by the commonality of the spirit of black consciousness.

Africa is the hope of humankind, it is the future of humanity. It would be essential to take a better view of this collective home country seen by many outside it as a single country, believed by few to be the runt of all civilisations, but in reality and in all fairness, it is the only subject made of humanity and its identity of manifestation.

The next generation of Africans are already warming up to it, not sure about where we are going but comfortable about the efforts made to make our own mark's known. We are forever grateful to the ancient world for all the sacrifices they made to leave us a unique sense of history, be it worthy or unworthy. What makes us remarkable humanity is the history we have left behind, it would not be the aim of this conversation to address the issue of worthiness, what there remains to be addressed is the usefulness of our collective goal in paying lots of regards and respect to where we are coming from, thousand years from the golden sun.

Our history is our greatest strength, our self-esteem lies thereof, for therein stands the same ideological nature which has defined the truth we are seeking.

In a thousand years from now, children of the descendants of this ancient unity shall still walk these paths, in a few more years to come what we have done already will be remembered and celebrated in full, what we seek to inspire is the desire to strive for the golden path or the path to truth, a mission which has defined countless generations of Africans even the ones before us.

Africa shall still be here no matter what, Africa will be occupied by our offspring, in honour and adoration for the little work we have done given the limited time, agriculture shall be our hallmark, the world shall hit 10 billion or 12 billion people sooner than later. We think we will grow and generate tons of food to feed those several billions of people. Twelve billion stomachs with 24 billion feet all walking the sun-scorched paths of the earth, Africa will play a significant role in this regard, with an increase in technical capacity and technological advancement in all areas of human life, and for this Africa's children are preparing.

There shall be no room unturned, an increase in output will equal an increase in capacity, a gradient very critical to weigh the average value of growth in production and consumption, with this capacity of arable land, with a desire to cultivate this capacity and the drive to make a difference. We are held together as a means to an end, and an end to a tool. Not only do we agree to play a significant role in this project, but we are also expected to lead and bear the torch for humanity.

This is bestowed upon us, as we enter into the stuff we are made of, a desire to be outstanding and forthright, everything the black world and many more is known for, the northern part of Africa is already a desired destination for several who know it, and the black race of Africa are equally in tow, no one is left behind as the race hits up and bears it all.

It will be told in full and in part that everyone contributed their part to inspire this new world which unfolds unto us. Our relevance is made known not just by our self but by the significant increase in our positional role as a continent blessed with abundance, we are the hope of the future, and we must be ready when that call is made, we must be prepared when that mantle is thrust into our care, be it as a leader holding the mantle or as a leader urging everyone to the finish line.

Agriculture shall play a dignified role in the new world, and our relevance is unmistakable here, saddled with the unique responsibility of holding the realms of the humans as its circumstances begin to manifest itself, so shall what makes us a dignified race manifest its purpose in the light of truth.

I have seen a few who understand this line of thought, and I have seen a smaller few who can even dare think about it, but I must commend those very true minds who are confident of our front and are even committed to lending voices to this call, we have made the need to answer the call greater than the call itself. No one dares to ask these types of questions, for the best of this world and the world to come is already upon us.

One November morning, during the closing session of a seminal meeting, I closed my arguments about Africa's future with the point that we need not be too worried about ourselves. We have existed on our own terms, we had technology which helped us make our daily lives better, we had developed along the lines of what everyday life and its challenges are thrown our way, that way we did what was demanded or required of us, the environment we found ourselves however brutish and raw made us into a very robust species of humans. This is not an argument that our technology or our life was or is the best, in fact, I haven't yet seen any country or continent whose own technology is the best of all technology, I haven't seen anyone, in particular, be it an individual or a group whose life is better than the other.

In several years of reading and continuously making inquisitive incursions into what relates to the life we led back then during those monolithic ages or the Stone Age, I have learned to understand that each research case should be considered mutually exclusive from the other. By this conversation, one civilisation should not be judged by yet another society, however, we can as a matter of principle look at the areas of improvement or the actions of these different ways of life that made it more understandably sustainable to inspire progress.

Having said this, I will draw parallels with idealism and realism here, having in mind that what one considers to be true about life may not in a real sense reflect the same in thought. I will suggest a closer relationship between the subject matter, wherein, the connection between humanity is thoroughly rooted and looked at in the efforts to understand what makes us manifest ourselves in ways that make us all different.

I am not constrained to continue with efforts to seek the truth, but I am happy to make my points known here that there are several occasions whereby it would be reckless not to accept the assurances of the truth that we are the essence of creativity and the source of collective consciousness.

The greatest tragedy of Africa lies in the band of the Africans themselves, contrary to popularly held opinions or beliefs of the international community that Africa is besieged by famine, civil war, poverty, poor governance, lack of quality leadership, poor infrastructure, lack of sustainable economic growth, unqualified or substandard quality of education, disease and several other known and unknown challenges, we believe that Africa's most traumatic experience lies in the divided minds of the young and the old, the educated and the uneducated, and lastly the battle between those who are led and those who are leading.

We have since agreed to this effect chiefly because in our several years of existence the most extraordinary good Africa has done to itself is its ability to accept that it has done far below its limitations, in inspiring hopes for its own development.

Those who picture the world differently from others may have seen things differently, hence should not be considered a threat or unconventional to the truth, every opinion should count, and all areas of thought and conversations should be tolerated. This is the truth hidden in plain sight.

The next big thing is potentially African, the next possible decision for Africans is the dire need to reposition itself in ways never before seen. A reflection of what needed to be done in the first place, and the zeal to play a significant role in the new world, I have seen lots of contrary thoughts concerning this possibility, a development which is crucial and vital but sadly unrecognised by a vast majority of folks in Africa.

We are doing ourselves a great disservice if we are not available to this new trend, we should make ourselves open for the transition from the former to the latter.

Our future is secured and brighter, there is no doubt about it here, or anywhere else, our share of the world is still in our hands. However, several other scholars have argued in opposition, the truth is that the future belongs to no particular nation, individual or group in particular, what then remains is for us as a people to position ourselves in the best ways possible to take advantage of the situation when the need arises.

This we must not fail to do; otherwise, our position would be further complicated or compounded, development may not be necessarily measured in terms of output and inputs, the reality is that a trend which has the potentials to transform itself into the next best or the possible best needs to be availed the opportunity to manifest itself.

Measured in co-referential terms, development is continuous, and change is the earth's most recognisable constant, time and time again it has manifested itself in as many ways possible, making it almost impossible for one to overlook or isolate.

Our teeming youth population is forever vibrant and creative, Africa is blessed and vested with some of the brightest talents known to humankind-writers, artists, musicians, doctors, lawyers, engineers, thinkers, computer scientists, entrepreneurs and a vast majority of talented individuals fit into this narrative.

Ostensibly, Africa is not in competition with "Europe" in any way, it is the cradle of ancient human forms, its most profound strength lies in its weakness, which is underscored by several years of misinformation and then the unhealthy leadership practices of most of its elites.

The ever-present words of another African great mind best begins to describe this reality. Chinua Achebe, although in memories continues to call the African spirit to action, he says, "Nobody can teach me who I am, and what I need is something I have to find myself." Lofty thoughts from late Novelist and Literary Icon whose works helped to redefine the long-held wrong stereotypes about Africa.

Ever pondered on these words, "I dream of an Africa which is in peace with itself."-the words of another African legend, this time in the person of South Africa's first black president and African National Congress leader, Dr Nelson Mandela, one of the most outstanding leaders to have emerged from Africa and a global statesman.

In reality, there is no easier way to comprehend this noble quest or even broaden its application. The best form of thought is best contained in the unique view shared by folks with discerning minds. Knowledge can be intimidating; intelligence can be a threat to those who do not aspire to it but the greatest undoing of mankind is the idea not to embrace the search. The worst of all wrongdoing would be to distance our mind from knowledge or confine our thoughts to the locked audience of mediocrity, that we must endeavour to avoid by all means possible, it is the pillars to which the twin cast shadows on humanity and humankind has evolved.

Let me also please make a reminder here, more like a remark that if we allow the ability to seek, or the intent to search to intimidate us or others, we have failed ourselves already. What makes us an extraordinary continent of warriors and seekers is the ancient commitment to seek and search for what best explains who we are to ourselves from which the rest of the world has lit its torch.

The battle line has been drawn between the need to seek and the determination not to inspire. To continue to this day, information and knowledge have always led us to discover things that our self-conscious comforts would never sanction, that inner consciousness to not explore, that tiny little voice inside our head which continually speaks of the need to conserve or hold steady, that internal call which discourages the spirit from seeking and searching for the truth.

To make sense of humanity and its affinity with the old world of Africa, we must think through the mind's most enormous and most spread-out fog of the time, a cloud which beckons on all who aspire to accept the remote nodes of thoughts scattered around and across the length of the surface of the earth.

As the era of inquisition and curiosity enters a new phase, and as the number of seekers to the truth extends across Africa and its own difficulties, spreading all along the hills of Drakensberg, the apex of the Rwenzori Mountains, Atlas Mountains tops. All through the Ethiopian Highlands extending towards the Virunga Mountains-a chain of volcanoes in East Africa, foreshadowing the ancient civilisation of Giza, in Egypt-the Sphinx and the Pyramids, in the south the watershed curtains of the Victoria falls, the lake Victoria itself and several other landmarks that are identified by our collective history surrounding the Horn of Africa. The Horn of Africa is typically the iconic peninsula and the easternmost elevation of the African continent. A steep line which lies along the southern corners of the Red Sea and stretches a few hundreds of kilometres into the area of the Gulf of Aden, overlooking the Somali Sea and the Guardafui Channels, a geographic definition which has made us manifest in more ways than envisioned in terms of human civilisation. Africa and its children will thrive in the new world, and they will not just succeed but will soar high above.

As I write this book's final words, a heavy dark cloud weighs upon my heart even as I am determined to be optimistic about the future of the world's children. Reading through the State of the World Children report by Unicef a while ago, the report revealed that children are surviving and not thriving in the world today. While the west battles obesity, the rest of the world and especially Africa suffers from a lack of access to food and clean water even in a world where more than enough food is produced to go around.

By not solving a simple fundamental physiological problem like hunger, how can we then solve all the other issues that prevent children from across the world to join the butterfly generation, a generation of children in which there is no restriction to the fulfilment of their deeply buried potential? An age that is not threatened by the environment but who are taught to be stewards of it. A generation that is not discriminated against because of their gender, colour, or sexual orientation. A generation that takes on the information revolution of the 21st-century head-on. And a generation capable of seeing not only beyond the religion-coloured lenses but through their minds' education to peacefully coexist. How can we accomplish these when these children are not even fed? How can we? This means that so far, we can keep the bottom half of children alive but not well enough to experience their lives with passion and maximise their potential while that magic place called childhood still dwells within them. But I always choose to cling to hope- the kind that I see in the eyes of children. They are my teachers.

In a world of space and time, when you talk of the future, you can be sure that its purest form can only germinate from a child's mind. What future are we talking about? The future where every child has a beautiful chance at life, à la carte. Children often have stronger will-power than adults, a doubtless disposition to life and a very optimistic expectation on life except when they run out of candies. It would be great if we could replace the nightmares, and horrid images, that makes the children in Africa and other continents of the world cry, lose limbs, lose family, and lose hope amidst the violence the nations of the world deliver to them. Children do not care about the reasons behind the world's conflicts, but we do because we are the perpetrators behind the wild storms. Looking at the positive paradigm of living through this thing called life which every child is born into and with efforts from you targeted at saving the future of every one of these beautiful kids, maybe they will even get candy after all.

AFTERWORD

When I was younger, as a little boy growing up on the streets of Northern Nigeria, I saw things from the point of view of the singular nature.

As an adult who is grown into a man still in the same country, I saw things a lot more in complex ways, or simply put in a multitude of different ways.

I saw Nigeria as a country where everything we did was all about us, nothing else compared to it, in a way that made common sense possible. Then, several times over the past came calling, coup d'états, periodically held elections that only served a few sets of political leaders, this led to massive protests and civil demonstrations, aired daily on national television, when it pleased those who care to allow it broadcast.

We felt the heat, as things began to disentangle and eventually disintegrate, as one strong man successful succeeded another strong man, the vicious cycle was endless, each strong man worked tirelessly to undo the foolishness of his predecessor, I watched, we all watched in our houses especially as children as the ancestors took turns to abandon us to our fate, we were doomed.

Several years later, I saw in Europe, a continent I had viewed as different, where everything made sense in the context of common sense, a place where everything was done for purposes other than the bizarre, or so I felt at that point. Why are they different? I queried, as I continually took turns to enquire about the things that stood us apart in ways that made sense to us as children. Why we spoke out loudly on top of our noses and why it looks like Europeans spoke through their nose or underneath it, as a child in my form would put it, the windpipes, sounded aloof and high like a pointedly cracked microphone.

Well, it took me several more years to see things differently from the years of my childhood, differently, in that sense was not always seen from the common-sense point of view, everyone and everything that we see owns its definition from the existence of the society it functions.

My childhood was very good and different from my adulthood, I have had cause to go back memory lane to ask questions I had the urgency to ask as a child now even as an individual person, the adult who grew up from the urgent questions of the past from the lenses of a little boy growing up in Northern Nigeria, its largely primordial political structures, its ancient philosophy of modern civilization, its ability to rally itself into action against the demands of the secular needs of the society, especially from within the conceptual cultural and institutional diversities of the mixed nationhood of Nigeria.

Interestingly, the story continues. It is a lot more than I can discuss here now as an adult, and a lot more as a child, but one thing stands out here, the chapters you just saw in a way redefines my thoughts as a child, whose only preoccupation was based on the immediate elementary assumptions and considerations of the society I found myself in, guarded, guided and organized to make sense to everyone else in a way a child would make little sense of it, that society continues to ask the type of questions that I probably asked then as a child, and yet as with a scope who dedicated itself to observe issues in a way that made it primarily impossible for the developed mind to comprehend. I find it fundamentally difficult to understand why things are happening the way they are.

Beards Don't Grow in Heaven, tactically and empirically has influenced me and in doing so has structurally answered some of the questions about my childhood experiences, things I have struggled to respond to even in my better understanding of the world as an adult.

Whether or not Heaven is real, or beards actually grow on its human population, real or imagined, this title has inspired a new and conscious conversation in my head about the likelihood that some things I became aware of as an adult may not be the same as the things I saw as a child back in northern Nigeria.

In comparative context, I will continue with my own difficulties in this new line of thought, soaking up the entire thought process to myself and believing in the power of awakening, that sometime soon, some of the questions answered here and some other questions equally raised here will find the path to a worthy source of merit.

To imply to this point rhetorically, if "Beards" were allowed to Grow in Heaven, then it becomes an imaginary problem that will engage us more in ways we can not relate with.

Chì NDù ÈfóGò, Poet & Storyteller, Love in the Eyes of a Widow & Oh Son of Dust.

University of Port Harcourt, Nigeria.

ACKNOWLEDGEMENTS

I would like to acknowledge the enormous debt of gratitude I owe my Editor, Teddy Celestine Inieke, whose support and vision made this book ready enough to be released to the world like a message in a bottle washed ashore. Without Teddy's keen eyes, Beards Don't Grow in Heaven would not have been made as readable as it presently is.

Although she may not remember anymore, I most profoundly would like to thank Cheri Pies, professor emeritus of

Maternal, Child and Adolescent Health at the UC Berkeley School of Public Health, University of California, Berkeley, for nudging me to complete this work just when the desire to throw it in the trash had me consumed. I am glad to have met her when I did during a coffee break at the Columbia Global Center at Rue de Chevreuse, Paris. Her faith in the story I had to share with the world sparked a flame in my heart and set my feet steadily on the path of a hasty completion of this book.

My writing path crossed that of Chì NDù ÈfóGò, a formidable African renaissance writer in every sense of the word who has also become a dear friend and, even more than anything, a solid trellis that sprouts vines of solid support on my writing. I conversed with him several times while scribbling down the words in this book, and he never for once felt irritated by my invasion of his time, which I imagined interrupted his writing. I thank him warmly, and I remain hugely indebted my dear friend.

Many of the thoughts expressed in this book were developed in late-night conversations after dinner with my Dad, Dr Audu Emmanuel Itodo. While he still breathed life, he was one of the most liberal and wise men I know who have graced the surface of this universe in the rare dance of the elements in this experience called life. For the thick doses of philosophical wisdom, he often provided me with a dash of humour both in words and action, I remain forever thankful. I must be fortunate because I have never seen anyone who believes so much in me like my mum, Victoria Onyeche Itodo. She can keep her tender heart guiding me gently like the Pole Star in my journey of growth even when we have divergent belief systems like a forked path in the woods. She remains the strongest woman that I know, and it is a precious gift of nature to have been nurtured under her wings and watchful eyes. I am grateful for her genuine love and constant support.

Life is about shared experiences that nurture our spirit. I can't resound my thanks enough to my siblings for persuading me to complete this book through their deliberate inquisition on the progress of the manuscript or through their beautiful lives that made me thankful for the gift of a family and for the shared experiences we created growing up and playing together which shaped my perception of life.

Many of these experiences have come to be expressed in my life in a completely different way than what we initially experienced. Still, I believe this is due to the transformative process that life performs on raw materials. Thank you,

Patrick, Kennedy, Victor, Precious, and Ema. I thank Victor for keeping me awake several times at my writing desk by his tendency to ask constantly when the last word in this book would be written.

Every human deserves the company of warm friends as they voyage through the complex cave crevices that life seems to be. First, friends can serve as spotless mirrors from which we can look at the reflections we project to the world. Secondly, I have heard it said that when a human has nowhere to lay their head, it is often in the spare room of their friend's home that they are given a second chance to be reborn in phoenix-like regeneration. In this light, I would like to thank my friends Richard Asekunowo and Godson Uzor for their kind-heartedness and for the way they keep on challenging me to reveal a better version of myself each day. I am grateful to have as friends Dr Felix Ubani with whom I face the world better, Kamara Abishai Bature, Aminu Musa, Dr Julfa Timkuk and Johnpaul Nnamdi. You all keep on inspiring me to leave good behind and sail for excellence.

Finally, most importantly, I thank every child of the world for holding on and waiting patiently while we, mostly clueless adults, try to stem the tide that threatens to flood their world.

We are getting better, and the future must be secured for them, for in their hands will the reins of economic progress, global peace, justice, and a safe planet be placed.

Oche Itodo, born in 1989, is a Nigerian epidemiologist, humanist, and human rights activist. For his efforts in challenging the death penalty in his country, and for volunteering and rallying for women and children estranged from the health grid in his country, he was bestowed an honour by France's foremost Institut français, Paris (Labcitoyen) in 2013.

Oche publishes creative articles on www.ocheitodo.com and writes on a diverse and wide range of topics covering human rights, public health, and global development on his blog, www.humanityspring.com. He currently resides across France and Switzerland. Beards don't grow in heaven is his first book.

Thank you!!!

I want to specially thank you the reader, for coming along on this explorative ride. *I hope you had as much fun as I did. If so, please take a moment to post a review on the platform where you purchased this book from and tell a friend.*

You can also keep in touch with me by following my facebook, twitter and Instagram pages using my username (@ocheforsure)

If you would like to stay updated on my projects and be informed first on future releases, you can sign up for my newsletter through this link: https://ocheitodo.com/news-letter/

BIBLIOGRAPHY:

1. KHALID, S., Nigeria's educational crisis: The almajiranci system and social realities. Islamic culture 2001, 75 (3), 85-103.

2. Amzat, J., Lumpen childhood in Nigeria: A case of the Almajiri in Northern Nigeria. Islamic Culture 2001, 85 (3), 85-103.

3. UNESCO New Methodology Shows that 258 Million Children, Adolescents and Youth Are Out of School.

http://uis.unesco.org/sites/default/files/documents/new-methodology-shows-258-million-children-adolescents-and-youth-are-out-school.pdf (accessed 20 march, 2020).

4. Isaacson, W., Einstein: His life and universe. Simon and Schuster: New York, 2007; p 865.5. Amy Damon.; Paul Glewwe.; Suzanne Wisniewski.; Sun, B. Education in developing countries: what policies and programmes affect learning and time in school?; 2016.

6. Sahlberg, P.; Ravitch, D.; Hargreaves, A.; Robinson, K., Finnish lessons 2.0 what can the world learn from educational change in Finland? 2015.

7. HRW Africa: Make Girls' Access to Education a Reality. End Exclusion from School for Married, Pregnant Students.https://www.hrw.org/news/2017/06/16/africa-make-girls-access-education-reality#:~:text=More%20than%2049%20million%20girls,rights%20and%20limiting%20their%20opportunities.&t

ext=In%2014%20sub%2DSaharan%20

countries,birth%20before%20they%20are%2018.

8. Adebowale, A. S., Ethnic disparities in fertility and its determinants in Nigeria. Fertility Research and Practice 2019, 5 (1), 3.

9. Unicef Girls' education: A lifeline to development; United Nations Children's Fund: 1996.

10. Liu, C.-R.; Liang, H.; Zhang, X.; Pu, C.; Li, Q.; Li, Q.-L.; Ren, F.-Y.; Li, J., Effect of an educational intervention on HPV knowledge and attitudes towards HPV and its vaccines among junior middle school students in Chengdu, China. BMC Public Health 2019, 19 (1), 488.

11. Fayoyin, A., The menace of VVF in Nigeria. Niger Pop 1993, 6-7.

12. Jayachandran, S., The Roots of Gender Inequality in Developing Countries. Annual Review of Economics 2015, 7 (1), 63-88.

13. Rwafa, U., Culture and Religion as Sources of Gender Inequality: Rethinking Challenges Women Face in Contemporary Africa. Journal of Literary Studies 2016, 32 (1), 43-52.

14. Hammarberg, T. A School for Children with Rights: The significance of the United Nations Convention on the Rights of the Child for modern education policy.; International Child Development Centre, Florence: 1998.

15. Montoya, S. Data to Celebrate 50 Years of Progress on Girls' Education. http://uis.unesco.org/en/blog/data-celebrate-50-years-progress-girls-education (accessed 27 December).

16. Yousafzai, M., I am Malala : the schoolgirl who stood up to the Taliban. Orion Publishing Group: London, UK, 2013.

17. Somani, T., Importance of Educating Girls for the Overall Development of Society: A Global Perspective. Journal of Educational Research and Practice 2017, 7 (1), 125-139.

18. McNeish, H. Malawi's fearsome chief, terminator of child marriages. https://www.aljazeera.com/features/2016/5/16/malawis-fearsome-chief-terminator-of-child-marriages (accessed January 1st).

19. Varfolomeeva, A. Number

of child soldiers involved in conflicts worldwide jumps 159% in 5 years. https://www.thedefensepost.com/2019/02/11/child-soldiers-global-increase/ (accessed January 2).

20. Siviy, S. M., A Brain Motivated to Play: Insights into the Neurobiology of Playfulness. Behaviour 2016, 153 (6-7), 819-844.

21. Andreu Cabrera, E.; Cepero, M.; Rojas, F. J.; Chinchilla-Mira, J. J., Play and childhood in ancient greece. 2010 2010, 5 (3), 9.

22. Geneva), U. C. o. H. R. t. s. Convention on the Rights of the Child; 1990.

23. Children, S. t., CHILDREN AFFECTED BY ARMED CONFLICT IN AFRICA CALL ON GOVERNMENTS TO TAKE ACTION TO PROTECT MOST VULNERABLE. Save the Children: 2019; Vol. 2021.

24. Ngo, A. D.; Taylor, R.; Roberts, C. L.; Nguyen, T. V., Association between Agent Orange and birth defects: systematic review and meta-analysis. Int J Epidemiol 2006, 35 (5), 1220-30.

25. Stuart Lester., W. R. Children's right to play:An examination of the importance of play in the lives of children worldwide.; The Hageue, The Netherlands: Bernard van Leer Foundation, 2010.

26. Dadvand, P.; Gascon, M.; Markevych, I., Green Spaces and Child Health and Development. In Biodiversity and Health in the Face of Climate Change, Springer, Cham: 2019; pp 121-130.

27. reporter, D., The oldest gay in the village: 5,000-year-old is 'outed' by the way he was buried. Daily mail online 2011.

28. Murray, S. O., Homosexuality in 'Traditional' Sub-Saharan Africa and Contemporary South Africa-an overview 1999.

29. Hoff, B. H., Gays: Guardians of the Gates: An Interview with Malidoma Somé. 1993.

30. HRW Children Behind Bars: The Global Overuse of Detention of Children; Human Rights Watch: 2016.

31. Wikipedia Oscar Wilde. https://en.wikipedia.org/wiki/Oscar_Wilde#Imprisonment (accessed 19th September).

32. Berliner, A. K., Sex, Sin,

and the Church: The Dilemma of Homosexuality. Journal of Religion and Health 1987, 26 (2), 137-142.

33.   Hooker, E., The adjustment of the male overt homosexual. J Proj Tech 1957, 21 (1), 18-31.

34.   Harari, Y. N., Sapiens : a brief history of humankind. 2018.

35.   LeVay, S., Gay, straight, and the reason why the science of sexual orientation. 2017.

36.   Yamanouchi, K., Mounting and lordosis behavior in androgen primed ovariectomized rats: effect of dorsal deafferentation of the preoptic area and hypothalamus. Endocrinol Jpn 1980, 27 (4), 499-504.

37.   Wikipedia List of animals displaying homosexual behavior. https://en.wikipedia.org/w/index.php?title=List_of_animals_displaying_homosexual_behavior&oldid=984144935 (accessed 21 November 2020 14:16 UTC).

38.   Brock, O.; Baum, M. J.; Bakker, J., The development of female sexual behavior requires prepubertal estradiol. J Neurosci 2011, 31 (15), 5574-8.

39.   Daae, E.; Feragen, K. B.; Waehre, A.; Nermoen, I.; Falhammar, H., Sexual Orientation in Individuals With Congenital Adrenal Hyperplasia: A Systematic Review. Front Behav Neurosci 2020, 14, 38.

40.   Loughlin, G., Catholic homophobia. Theology 2018, 121 (3), 188-196.

41.   Haggerty, G. E.; Zimmerman, B.; Beynon, J.; Haggerty, P. G. E.; Eisner, D., Gay Histories and Cultures: An Encyclopedia. Garland: 2000.

42.   Martel, F.; Whiteside, S., In the Closet of the Vatican. 2019.

43.   Callaghan, T. D.; van Leent, L., Homophobia in Catholic schools: An exploration of teachers' rights and experiences in Canada and Australia. Journal of Catholic Education 2019, 22, 36-57.

44.   Buckle, L. African sexuality and the legacy of imported homophobia. https://www.stonewall.org.uk/about-us/news/african-sexuality-and-legacy-imported-homophobia (accessed 29th November, 2020).

45.   Li, M. No Human Can Beat AlphaGo, and It's a Good Thing. https://towardsdatascience.com/no-

human-can-beat-alphago-so-what-3401b40fa0f0 (accessed 31 January, 2021).

46.   Doner, T. Why I taught myself 20 languages — and what I learned about myself in the process. https://ideas.ted.com/author/timothy-doner/ (accessed 02 February, 2021).

47.   Di Giacomo, D.; Ranieri, J.; Lacasa, P., Digital Learning As Enhanced Learning Processing? Cognitive Evidence for New insight of Smart Learning. Frontiers in Psychology 2017, 8 (1329).

48.   Lacy, A. d. 5G opens the future of telesurgery. https://healthmanagement.org/c/healthmanagement/issuearticle/5g-opens-the-future-of-telesurgery (accessed 04 February, 2021).

49.   Ito, J. Why Westerners Fear Robots and the Japanese Do Not. https://www.wired.com/story/ideas-joi-ito-robot-overlords/ (accessed 05 February, 2021).

50.   Nadotti, C. Daltonici, mondo a colori con l'aiuto di "Eyeborg". https://www.repubblica.it/2005/e/sezioni/scienza_e_tecnologia/daltonismo/daltonismo/daltonismo.html?ref=search (accessed 06 February, 2021).

51.   Cyranoski, D. The CRISPR-baby scandal: what's next for human gene-editing. https://www.nature.com/articles/d41586-019-00673-1 (accessed 07 February, 2021).

52.   Sorgner, S. L. In Nietzsche, the Overhuman, and Transhumanism, 2009.

53.   Seung, S., Connectome : how the brain's wiring makes us who we are. 2013.

54.   Nunez, C. What is global warming, explained. https://www.nationalgeographic.com/environment/global-warming/global-warming-overview/ (accessed 17th December).

55.   Gornitz, V., Ancient Cultures and Climate Change. In Encyclopedia of Paleoclimatology and Ancient Environments, Gornitz, V., Ed. Springer Netherlands: Dordrecht, 2009; pp 6-10.

56.   Ahdoot, S.; Pacheco, S. E., Global Climate Change and Children's Health. Pediatrics 2015, 136 (5), e1468-84.

57.   Pinfold, J. V.; Horan, N. J.;

Mara, D. D., Seasonal effects on the reported incidence of acute diarrhoeal disease in northeast Thailand. Int J Epidemiol 1991, 20 (3), 777-86.

58.   Kurane, I., The Effect of Global Warming on Infectious Diseases. Osong Public Health and Research Perspectives 2010, 1 (1), 4-9.

59.   Mbow, C., C. Rosenzweig, L.G. Barioni, T.G. Benton, M. Herrero, M. Krishnapillai, E. Liwenga, P. Pradhan, M.G. Rivera-Ferre, T. Sapkota, F.N. Tubiello, Y. Xu Food Security. In: Climate Change and Land: an IPCC special report on climate change, desertification, land degradation, sustainable land management, food security, and greenhouse gas fluxes in terrestrial ecosystems; Intergovernmental Panel on Climate Change: 2019; pp 437-550.

60.   UNDP, Transforming food and agriculture: Creating food security while fighting climate change. 2020.

61.   Pinker, S., The Better Angels of Our Nature Why Violence Has Declined. Penguin Group USA: 2012.

62.   Aremu, T.; Abraham, P., Herdsmen on the Move: The Burdens of Climate Change and Environmental Migration in Nigeria. In: Leal Filho W. (eds) Handbook of Climate Change Resilience. Springer, Cham. 2018, 1-11.

63.   Segovia-Mendoza, M.; Nava-Castro, K. E.; Palacios-Arreola, M. I.; Garay-Canales, C.; Morales-Montor, J., How microplastic components influence the immune system and impact on children health: Focus on cancer. Birth Defects Res 2020, 112 (17), 1341-1361.

64.   Parker, L. Plastic trash flowing into the seas will nearly triple by 2040 without drastic action. https://www.nationalgeographic.com/science/2020/07/plastic-trash-in-seas-will-nearly-triple-by-2040-if-nothing-done/ (accessed 20th December).

65.   Gajanan, M. Republican Congressman Says God Will 'Take Care Of' Climate Change. https://time.com/4800000/tim-walberg-god-climate-change/ (accessed 21 December).

66.   Daley, J. U.S. Exits Paris Climate Accord after Trump Stalls Global Warming Action for Four

Years.
https://www.scientificamerican.com/
article/u-s-exits-paris-climate-accord-
after-trump-stalls-global-warming-
action-for-four-years/ (accessed 21
December).

67.   Reilly, K. Pope Francis
Gave President Trump a Copy of His
Encyclical on Climate Change.
https://time.com/4792296/pope-
francis-donald-trump-climate-change-
encyclical/ (accessed 21 December).

68.   DW Auschwitz Memorial
director offers to share Nigerian boy's
blasphemy jail term.
https://www.dw.com/en/auschwitz-
memorial-director-offers-to-share-
nigerian-boys-blasphemy-jail-term/a-
55065522 (accessed 21 January, 2021).

69.   Lantos, H.; Wilkinson, A.;
Winslow, H.; McDaniel, T.,
Describing associations between child
maltreatment frequency and the
frequency and timing of subsequent
delinquent or criminal behaviors
across development: variation by sex,
sexual orientation, and race. BMC
Public Health 2019, 19 (1), 1306.

70.   Taylor, M. P.; Forbes, M.
K.; Opeskin, B.; Parr, N.; Lanphear, B.
P., The relationship between
atmospheric lead emissions and
aggressive crime: an ecological study.
Environ Health 2016, 15, 23.

71.   Harris, S., Free will. Free
Press/Simon & Schuster: London,
2012.

72.   Ling, S.; Umbach, R.;
Raine, A., Biological explanations of
criminal behavior. Psychol Crime Law
2019, 25 (6), 626-640.

73.   Batrinos, M. L.,
Testosterone and aggressive behavior
in man. Int J Endocrinol Metab 2012,
10 (3), 563-8.

74.   Hoskin, A. W.; Ellis, L.,
Fetal testosterone and criminality:
Test of evolutionary neuroandrogenic
theory. Criminology 2015, 53 (1), 54-
73.

75.   WHO Lead poisoning and
health. https://www.who.int/news-
room/fact-sheets/detail/lead-
poisoning-and-health (accessed 27
January, 2021).

Made in the USA
Monee, IL
07 July 2026